An Introduction to
SOCIAL ANTHROPOLOGY

By the Same Author

AN INTRODUCTION TO ANTHROPOLOGICAL THOUGHT
AN INTRODUCTION TO INDIAN ANTHROPOLOGY

An Introduction to
SOCIAL ANTHROPOLOGY

(A Textbook for the students of Anthropology, Sociology & I.A.S. Examinees)

MAKHAN JHA, PH.D., D.LITT.
Professor of Anthropology
U.G.C. Centre of Advanced Study,
Department of Anthropology
Ranchi University, Ranchi (India)

VIKAS PUBLISHING HOUSE PVT LTD

VIKAS PUBLISHING HOUSE PVT LTD
576, Masjid Road, Jangpura, **New Delhi**-110 014
Phones: 4314605, 4315313 • Fax: 91-11-4310879
Email: *chawlap@giasdl01.vsnl.net.in* • Internet: *www.ubspd.com*

First Floor, N.S. Bhawan, 4th Cross 4th Main
Gandhi Nagar, **Bangalore**-560 009 • Phone : 2204639

F-20, Nand Dham Industrial Estate, Marol,
Andheri (East), **Mumbai**-400 059 • Phone : 8502333

Distributors:
UBS PUBLISHERS' DISTRIBUTORS LTD
5, Ansari Road, **New Delhi**-110 002
Ph. 3273601, 3266646 • Fax : 3276593, 3274261
E-mail: *ubspd.del@smy.sprintrpg.ems.vsnl.net.in* • Internet: *www.ubspd.com*
- 10, First Main Road, Gandhi Nagar, **Bangalore**-560 009 • Ph. 2263901
- 6, Sivaganga Road, Nungambakkam, **Chennai**-600 034 • Ph. 8276355
- 8/1-B, Chowringhee Lane, **Calcutta**-700 016 • Ph. 2441821, 2442910
- 5-A, Rajendra Nagar, **Patna**- 800 016 • Ph. 672856, 656169
- 80, Noronha Road, Cantonment, **Kanpur**-208 004 • Ph. 369124, 362665

Distributors for Western India:
PREFACE BOOKS
Shivali Apartments, Plot no. 1, 25/4 Chintamani Co-operative
Housing Society, Karve Nagar, **Pune**-411 052 • Ph. 315122

Copyright © Makhan Jha, 1994

First Edition, 1994
Second Reprint, 1999

All rights reserved. No part of this publication may be reproduced
in any form without the prior written permission of the publishers.

Information contained in this book has been published by VIKAS Publishing
House Pvt. Ltd. and has been obtained by its authors from sources believed
to be reliable and are correct to the best of their knowledge. However, the
publisher and its authors shall in no event be liable for any errors, omissions
or damages arising out of use of this information and specifically disclaim
any implied warranties or merchantability or fitness for any particular use.

Printed at Vishal Printers, Delhi - 110 032

Preface

Social Anthropology is a compulsory paper for the students of Central Services. Wherever anthropology is taught in Indian universities or abroad, Social Anthropology is taught as a compulsory paper for which there was no text book since long. Although there were some old books on Social Anthropology, written by foreign scholars, but all of them are out of print for the last three decades. Further, Social Anthropology is also taught in sociology and hence this book—*An Introduction to Social Anthropology* has been written keeping in view the requirements of the students of Anthropology, Sociology and the examinees of I.A.S.

In the curriculum of Social Anthropology meant for the examinees of the Central Services, there is a chapter on "Field Work Traditions in Anthropology" for which there was no book available anywhere and hence I have added that chapter specially meant for the students of Central Services. Thus, all the latest information concerning either social anthropology or methods meant for the I.A.S. students have been incorporated in this book and I, therefore, hope that this volume will be highly useful for the students of Anthropology, Sociology and examinees of the Central Services.

For writting this book I collected a good deal of information last year when I was in Providence College, Rhode Island, U.S.A. for a short visiting assignment for which I am grateful to Professor Dr. Leslie Ellen Straub, O.P. and other academic staff of the College.

Ranchi   MAKHAN JHA
1st March, 1994

Contents

Preface   v

I. **Meaning and Scope of Anthropology and it's Main Branches**   1
Definitions of anthropology; Main branches; Physical anthropology; Social and Cultural anthropology; Archaeological anthropology; Anthropological Linguistic; Applied anthropology.

II. **Concepts of Community, Society and Culture**   17
Social Structures; Social organisation; Community and Society; Institution; Association; Social group; Band and Tribe; Social norms and social values; Culture and civilization; Social change.

III. **Marriage and Family in Primitive Societies**   39
It's concepts and definitions; Characteristics of marriage; Functions of marriage; Forms of marriage; Ways of acquiring mates; Rules of marriage; Marriage payments.
Concepts of family; Definitions of family; Functions and types of family; Stability and changes in the family.

IV. **Kinship System**   77
Type of kin group; Kinship behaviours—Joking and avoidance relationship; Couvade; Avunculate; Amitate; Teknonymy; Moiety, phratry, and clan; Rules of descent; Degree of Kinship; Rules of residence.

CONTENTS

V. Economic Anthropology — 94
Meaning and scope; Definitions and characteristics of primitive economy; Production and consumption in tribal economy; Mode of exchange—barter and ceremonial; Tribal market and trade; Primitive money; Characteristics of primitive money; Classifications of primitive money; Origin of primitive money.

VI. Political Anthropology — 112
Meaning and concepts; Definitions of primitive law; Difference between customs and law; Social sanction in primitive law; Structure of the primitive government in tribal society; Difference between state and stateless political system; Justice and punishments in primitive society; Nation building process in a state.

VII. Anthropology of Religion — 125
Meaning and scope; Definitions of primitive religion; Theory of religion; Tylor's theory of animism; Max Muller's theory of naturalism; The theory of Manaism; Functional theory of religion; Durkheim's concepts of sacred and profane; Difference between magic, religion and science; Differences between magic and science; Difference between magic and religion; Totem and taboo.

VIII Field Work and Field Work Traditions in Anthropology — 143
Importance of field work in anthropology; Field work traditions in anthropology; Approaches in anthropological field work; Field methods in anthropology; Interview, Observation, Genealogical table, Schedule and Questionnaire, Census and Survey, Sampling, Photographic and Cartographic methods, Psychological methods, Formal Semantic analysis method, Contents analysis method; Definition of hypothesis and methodology; Creation of rapport in field work; Review of literatures on field methods.

Bibliography — 163

Index — 166

CHAPTER I

Meaning and Scope of Anthropology and its Branches

The word "anthropology" has been derived from two Greek words, *anthropos* (man) and *logus* (study or science). Anthropology is, thus, the science of man. This etymological meaning, of course, is too broad and general. More precisely it may be called "the science of man and his works and behaviour".

Anthropologists are interested in all aspects of the human species and human behaviour, in all places and at all times, from the origin and evolution of the species through its prehistoric civilizations, down to the present situation.

Anthropologists study human behaviour not concerned with particular men as such, but with men in "groups", with races and peoples and their happenings or doings. So anthropology may be defined briefly as the "science of groups of men and their behaviour and productions". This will include any findings on the total human species, since this constitutes an aggregate of races or peoples, or a sort of super-group or total society.

Kluckhohn, a famous American anthropologist, has argued that out of all the sciences which study various aspects of man, anthropology is the one which comes nearest to being a total study of man. Anthropology studies man and his contemporary society, his past, and also his sub-human and pre-human origins; it studies man irrespective of whether he is primitive or civilized. Thus, it studies man at all levels of culture. Kluckhohn, thus, is right when he compares anthropology to a mirror in which man, without any labels of primitive or civilized, may look to understand his physical and cultural complexities. Similarly, Herskovits has concluded (1952) that anthropology is the study of *Man and his works* (the name of his famous book).

In 1876, Topinard gave a definition of anthropology, as quoted by Haddon (1934) and according to which anthropology is a branch of natural history and deals with man and the races of mankind. Thus, it is a historical study and reveals the development of man ever since his emergence about three-quarters of million years ago. It is quite natural then, that the physical emergence of man coincided with the development of his knowledge of stone tools and techniques. We then also come to know that some sort of social institutions have also existed right from the beginning and those social institutions have changed from time to time and have become more complex.

Franz Boas, the father of American anthropology, while writing an article on "Anthropology" in *Encyclopaedia of the Social Sciences* (Vol. II, 1930), said "anthropology deals with man as a social being". T.K. Penniman, in his book "A Hundred Years of Anthropology" (1935) has defined "anthropology as the science of man. In one aspect it is a branch of Natural History, and embraces the study of his origin and position in the realm of animated nature..... In another aspect, anthropology is the science of history".

Hoebel, in his book—"*Man in the Primitive World*" (1949) defines "anthropology as the study of man and all of his works", which is very similar to Kluckhohn's definition of anthropology. M. Jacobs and B. J. Stern, in their book "*General Anthropology*" (1955) have argued that "anthropology is the scientific study of the physical, social and cultural development and behaviour of human beings since their appearance on earth".

Anthropology is, thus, the study of emergence and development of man from physical, cultural and social points of view. Since it studies the physical emergence of man, the roots of anthropology as a science may be found in the natural sciences like biology, zoology, etc. The physical anthropologists of the 19th century mainly concentrated in studying the biological evolution of man. Charles Darwin's (1809-1882) early research is typical example of this approach. During his five-year voyage around the world (from 1831 to 1836), he gathered the information about animal varieties which ultimately enabled him to put together his idea about evolution.

The social and cultural anthropologists include a broad range of approaches derived from the social sciences like sociology, psychology, human-geography, economics, history, political science, etc. Anthropology is, thus, able to relate all of these disciplines to its quest for an understanding of human behaviour, and draws upon all of them to interpret the way in which all biological and social factors enter to depict the man's culture and behaviour in totality.

Branches of Anthropology

Anthropology may be conveniently divided into five broad sections, viz.,

  (i) Physical Anthropology
 (ii) Social & Cultural Anthropology.
(iii) Archaelogical Anthropology.
(iv) Linguistic Anthropology.
 (v) Applied Anthropology.

Each branch of anthropology studies one special aspect of human behaviour, and although each work separately with its own methods and its own subject matter, together they form a "whole" that is distinct from all other social services.

(i) Physical Anthropology
Physical anthropology is that branch concerned with own relationship to other animals, our derivation and evolution, and our special physical characteristics such as, mental capacity, shape of the band, erect posture, etc. In other words, physical anthropology studies human evolution and human variation. It is closely related to several of the natural sciences: zoology—in terms of the relationship to other animals and the overall place of the human species in the process of evolution; biology—in terms of the evolution of humans from early pre-human forms; anatomy and

physiology—in its concern with the structure of the human body, the relationship of the various parts, and the operation or function of these different parts; genetics—concern with variation in the world today; and even psychology—in the investigation of our mental make-up and its relationship to behaviour.

Physical anthropology considers the human species as a biological entity, as well as a social animal. Some physical anthropologists are concerned primarily with the past forms of pre-human and early human species, an area of study known as *fossil man*. Others concentrate on the similarities and differences between the various primate species, which include not only humans, but apes and monkeys as well. This area of study is called primatology. A third area, known as the study of human variation, or anthropological genetics, deals with contemporary as well as historical variations among populations of humans. It is concerned with questions such as the adaptation of a group of people to a specific climate, the natural immunity of some peoples to certain diseases, and the all-important questions of racial differences.

(ii) Social and Cultural Anthropology

(a) Social anthropology is called the natural science of society (Radcliffe Brown: 1952). This discipline of anthropology involves the comparative study of social systems and how they work? Social systems are the independent activities, institutions and values by which people live. It is the job of social anthropologists to identify the components of social systems and analyse their interdepence. As a school of thought (also called as primitive or *comparative sociology*) it was developed in England in the 1920's but its significance must be judged in terms of its antecedents.

(b) *Evolutionary Anthropology*:

The prevailing approach to anthropology, prior to the development of social anthropology, was evolutionary and comparative. Evolutionists started with the premise that society evolved everywhere along roughly similar lines from rudimentary beginnings through stages to its highest manifestations in different forms of civilization. It was the goal of evolutionary anthropologist to construct the history of social evolution through the detailed comparison of the customs of simpler and, thus, less evolved societies. Social anthropology was a reaction against this evolutionary tradition.

In the beginning the French sociologist, Emile Durkheim (1858-1917) had a decisive influence on the development of social anthropology. His work was based on the premise that social phenomena are autonomous and their relationships should be studied in their own right without reference to biology, geography or any other body of data or theory. A society, in Durkheim's view, is a system analogous to a biological organism which is sustained through the ordered interdependent functioning of its parts. It was the relationship between the parts within a society that was the proper study of sociology.

Following the principles of Durkheim, A.R. Radcliffe Brown (1881-1955) developed social anthropology in England. He embraced the organic model of society of Durkheim and explained the social institutions of Andamanese society (1922) by identifying their specific functions in maintaining the structure of that society. Because of their concern with the functional integration of social structure, Radcliffe Brown and his followers are often called structure-functionalists.

In the development of social anthropology, the Polish-born and English-trained anthropologist, Bronislaw Malinowski's (1884-1942) works and publications are very important. He developed functionalist approach of his own. Malinowski's functionalism was less true to Durkheimian principles than was Radcliffe Brown's. However, all later social anthropologists in England like E.E. Evans-Pritchard, Raymond Firth, E.R. Leach, S.F. Nadel, I. Schapera, etc., derived inspirations from the initial works of A.R. Radcliffe Brown and Bronislaw Malinowski, although later trends have added flexibility and dynamics to the various concepts of social anthropology, which will be discussed, in detail, later on in this book.

Social anthropology has been defined by many anthropologists and I quote some of them here, in brief, for the benefit of students.

According to Radcliffe Brown (1952), "Social anthropology

is that branch of sociology which deals with primitive or preliterate societies."

S.F. Nadel (1956) was of opinion that, "The primary object of social anthropology is to understand primitive peoples, the cultures they have created and the social system, in which they live and act."

E.E.Evans-Pritchard, a staunch supporter of A.R.Radcliffe Brown said (1951), "Social anthropology can be regarded as a branch of sociological studies, that branch which chiefly devotes itself to primitive societies."

G.P. Murdock, a noted American anthropologist, argued (1949) that "Social anthropology seems to me to be simply the branch of cultural anthropology that deals with interpersonal relationship." While in Encyclopaedia Britanica (vol. XX, p. 862) Social anthropology is "defined as one of the social sciences engaged in the comparative study of human societies."

Raymond Firth, a famous British anthropologist and a former student of Malinowski says (1951), "one of the broadest ways of describing social anthropology is to say that it studies human social process comparatively."

In his classical book—*An Introduction to Social Anthropology* (1952, Vol.I) Ralph Piddington pointed out that "Social Anthropologists study the cultures of contemporary primitive communities."

Among the Indian anthropologists, S.C. Dube and M.N. Srinivas have given very plausible definitions of social anthropology. S.C. Dube in his book—*Anthropology* (1952) says "Social anthropology is that part of Cultural anthropology, which devotes its primary attention to the study of social structure and religion rather than material aspect of culture".

M.N. Srinivas points out in a paper (Sociological Bulletin, Vol. I, No.I, 1952) that "It is a comparative study of human societies. Ideally it includes all societies—primitive, civilized and historic".

After going through all these definitions of social anthropology, one may conclude that it, no doubt, studies the contemporary primitive societies and the networks of their social relations but it falls within the greater ambit of cultural anthropology. In this connection it is further argued that social and cultural anthropology represents two traditions—while the former studies in terms of "societies", the latter refers to "culture". While social anthropology is the outcome of the impact of the Durkheimian school of thought, followed by the British anthropology, the cultural anthropology in the contemporary situation refers to the Americanisation of this discipline.

(b) *Cultural Anthropology:*

Like social anthropology, cultural anthropology has also been defined by various anthropologists, some of them are quoted below for the benefit of the students.

Beals and Hoijer, in their book—*Introduction to Anthropology* (1956), have said that "Cultural Anthropology studies the origins and history of man's cultures, their evolution and development, and the structure and functioning of human culture in every place and time". The famous American anthropologist M.J. Herkovits, in his book—*Man and His Works* (1955) has pointed out that "cultural anthropologists study the ways man has devised to cope with his natural setting and his social milieu, and how bodies of customs are learnt, retained and handed down from one generation to the next".

In their book—*General Anthropology* (1955), Jacobs and Stern suggest that "cultural anthropologists describe, analyse and attempt to account for the wide variety of customs and forms of social life of humans particularly of the people with primitive technologies."

Cultural anthropology, thus, as the term is commonly used today, generally refers to very wide field of studying the existing peoples. Further, it is based upon a comparative approach, that is, its main aim is to understand and appreciate the diversity in human behaviour, and ultimately to develop a science of human behaviour, through the comparison of different peoples through out the world.

As the subject matter of this discipline is very vast, one may include archaeology and anthropological linguistics under cultural anthropology, for they are both concerned with culture—the archaeologist with the cultures of pre-historic peoples and the linguist with a specific aspect of culture in both the past and the present. But since these subdisciplines are generally acknowledged to be separate from the major focus of cultural anthropology, it is better to accept this distinction.

Similarly, distinction is also made between two areas of cultural anthropology: *ethnology* and *ethnography*. Ethnology is the comparative study of culture and the investigation of theoretical problems using information about different groups. Ethnography is simply the description of one culture and not a comparative study. In other words, an ethnological study is based on two or more ethnographies; the latter form the raw materials for the former. However, in a very broad sense cultural anthropology is widely used for all such researches.

As stated earlier, the subject matter of cultural anthropology is very vast and precisely we may suggest that there are large number of *micro-theory* on which the foundations of this discipline rest.

Micro-theory in ethnology involves an interest in specific topic viewed in cross-cultural perspective. The micro-theory deals with overall patterns of cultural diversity and similarity.

A list of various micro-theories that constitute major sub-fields of cultural anthropology indicates the range of topics that interest the ethnologist: economic anthropology, which deals with economic organisation; anthropology of law, which considers social sanctions and conflict resolution; anthropology of religion; social organisation, specially the kinship systems of primitive groups; political anthropology; psychological anthropology, the study of personality in other societies; applied anthropology, in which anthropologists are concerned with introducing changes in other societies; peasantry; belief-system, the study of patterns of behaviour, which is further sub-divided into more specialised interests such as ethnobotany and ethnozoology; cultural ecology; complex societies, which includes such interests like urbanisation & industrialisation, pluralism and nationalism; medical anthropology; anthropology of education; anthropology of pilgrimage; demographic (population) anthropology; anthropology of recreation; ethnohistory; ethnomusicology; anthropology of dance, primitive art; folklore; culture change, etc. Each of these micro-theories focuses on one aspect of culture, which is the central theme of anthropology.

(iii) Archaeological Anthropology

Archaeology is an important branch of anthropology. Some- times it is also called as pre-history because it is concerned primarily with the early period of human existence, prior to the written records or historical accounts. The main aim of this branch of anthropology is to reconstruct the origin, spread and evolution of culture. It does this by examining the remains that we are fortunate enough to find of the past societies.

Archaeology is obviously related to history. Both archaeology and history attempt to reconstruct as much of the past as possible. However, the main difference between the two is this, that while history deals primarily with the written records of literate civilizations, archaeology goes back beyond where history begins reconstructing the past prior to the invention of scripts and writings.

The archaeologist assumes the same task as other kinds of anthropologists, in that he is also concerned with understanding as much as possible about human behaviour. The difference is that his materials are the unwritten records of past societies and he does not have the opportunity to sit down with living members of those societies and go over the various interpretations of what he finds. The archaeologist cannot observe living people, but must abstract from the remains of the past whatever he can. Thus, the main items to be examined by the archaeologists are the various stone implements and tools, weapons and other remains of the past societies.

In brief, it may be concluded that the archaeological anthropology offers an opportunity to look into the distant past of the human species and then their cultural complexities are reconstructed. Thus, without the help of archaeology, an anthropologist cannot study the culture in totality.

(iv) Anthropological Linguistic

The study of language, from an anthropological perspective, forms an important branch of this discipline. Of course, linguistics also exists as a separate subject, but the anthropologist who specialises in this area is particularly concerned with the relationship between language and cultural behaviour. Anthropologists interested in the study of language, consider language as a part of our social world.

One area of interest in anthropological linguistics deals with the origin of language. Another area of concentration deals with the role of language in the context of social behaviour. This is relatively a new field known as sociolinguistics, and it is concerned with how we use the language we speak (or the different forms of language).

(i) Language and Perception
One of the most interesting aspects of anthropological linguistics from the perspective of cultural anthropology is the study of how our language determines the way we order our universe.

This does not mean that people who speak different languages perceive things differently, but rather that they tend to arrange the things they perceive in different ways according to the language they speak. This is something that varies from one culture to another.

(ii) Language and Culture
A language can tell us a lot about what is important in a particular culture. For example, if we look at the vocabulary of a language we will find a great deal of elaboration in words describing certain phenomena, while in other areas there will not be any elaboration at all. The Eskimo language, for example, has a vocabulary rich in words describing details of the Arctic environment. In one Eskimo language there are 12 separate and unrelated words for wind and 22 words for snow. That means 22 different kinds of snow are recognised in the Eskimo culture.

Finally, another interesting aspect of the study of language by anthropologist deals with the way people learn their language. Since language conveys so much of the contents of the culture, it is important to know how new members of a group are taught language and thereby to understand how they are "socialised"—that is, how they are trained to be members of that cultural group. Understanding the process by which the training takes palce, and the medium in which it is transmitted, is a major goal of the anthropological linguistics.

(iii) Language and Reality
Although perception depends on the reception of stimuli originating from outside the person, these have no meaning for the person until he or she categorizes them. Categorization is the process whereby differing stimuli are identified by a person as being the same, i.e., belonging to the same class. The classes one uses to organise perceptions are called cognitive categories; the organising process is called cognition.

The cognitive categories at a person's disposal do not generate themselves spontaneously in his or her mind. They are acquired through the process of *enculturation*—the process through which a person masters a culture and learns to speak a particular language. Edward Sapir (1884-1934), the famous American Linguist-Anthropologist, holds the view that the vocabulary of a language is an encoding of that culture's cognitive categories. Stephen A. Tyler, in his edited Volume on *'Cognitive Anthropology'* (1969) has argued that the reality of a language is a socio-cultural product and hence relative.

(iv) New Ethnography
The New Ethnography, now more appropriately defined as cognitive anthropology, consists of a series of principles, approaches and data collecting procedures which share the assumption that culture consists of the knowledge one must know or believe in order to behave appropriately in a culture. It has a concern for the categories, plans, rules and organising principles of behaviour that a person has in his mind as a member of cultures. Generally, the New Ethnography, also known as ethnoscience, includes topics such as the emic/etic distinction, folk taxonomies, ethno semantic and componential analysis.

The New Ethnography approaches a culture from the perspective of a member of that culture. This point of view is, of course, not new, and goes back to the early years of anthropology. Several important differences, however, distinguish the new from the old ethnography.

First of all, the New ethnographers use the native

language itself as the data of the description rather than as just a tool to obtain the data.

Secondly, with their preoccupation with language as a data source, they tend to exclude the anthropologist's categorization of the non-verbal behaviour in the culture and use only the informant's description of such behaviour as data.

Thirdly, the New Ethnographers are concerned about obtaining an accurate record of the process of gathering the data.

Fourthly, some New Ethnographers assume that the question-response pair constitutes the basic unit of the informant's cognitive structure.

The fifth difference between the New Ethnography and the old varieties rests on the systematic approach to data collecting, which proceeds in a definite sequence. The advantage of this systematic approach to ethnography is twofold: Other anthropologists working in the same culture can theoretically reproduce the data, if they desire, by using the same techniques; more over, the data from several informants can easily be stored and organised by computers for analysis later. Reproducibility constitutes an important tenet of scientific research specially in the field of New Ethnography. This new approach, developed in the early 1960s in America, has gained popularity in the American anthropology.

(v) Applied Anthropology
In the broadest sense, this term refers to the use of anthropological concepts, methods, theories and findings for a specific purpose of solving the problems which confront the societies.

In the beginning the applied aspect of this science was not visualised. It was considered nothing more than a collection of colourful and spicy information regarding the queer and grotesque customs of the savages, by travellers and globetrotters. It read like romance and was of value because it satisfied human thirst for wonder and curiosity.

However, this phase passed very soon. Slowly the immense cultural significance of this science was realised. It helps us not only in reconstructing our cultural history, but it is also invaluable for the discovery and understanding of those universal social laws which govern all human societies. As such anthropology soon established itself as an important historical study.

In the meantime administrators, traders and missionaries were realising the possibilities of applying this knowledge to the solution of practical problems arising out of their contacts with primitive populations in their respective fields. It was felt that understanding and appreciation of anthropological facts could eliminate many conflicts and problems arising out of unnecessary misunderstanding. This could minimise tribal discomfort and heart-burning and smoothen the relationship between the rulers and the ruled. Gradually, the scope of applied anthropology widened and today it is beginning to claim that it can make a signifiant contribution for the solution of many tangled and baffling problems of racial tensions, cultural mal-adjustments and tribal administration.

To the student of social dynamics, as also to the practical social worker interested in the problems of welfare and social change, anthropology has much to offer. Cultures are not static, they are dynamic. But how do cultures change? What are the processes involved in the changes? A proper understanding of the dynamics of culture-change is invaluable for formulating plans to bring about smooth and speedy reforms in the patterns of tribal life. Anthropology can now claim to have developed a methodology of its own. These methods and techniques can be effectively used even for the study of the problems of population, nutrition and medical welfare. For making plans of economic welfare an understanding of the value system of a culture is very necessary. By using anthropological methods, we can easily analyse the structure of values accepted by a society.

In the direction of solving racial and minority problems, anthropology can claim the proud record of long and valiant fight against social superstition and selfishness. It has gone a long way in cleaning the mist of confusion and has aided the elimination of many of our racial prides and prejudices. It actually opens out before us the vast panorama of humanity and reveals so many different patterns of life and thought and knowledge of such a diversity of customs and institutions intimately helps us in solving their problems of socio-economic nature.

Applied Anthropology in India

In India the use of anthropology in running effective adminsitration was felt as early as in 1807 when the court of Directors of the East India Company made a formal decision that "such knowledge would be of great use in the future adminsitration of the country" (Roy, 1921). To carry out, thus, the formal decision of the East India Company, Francis Buchanan was appointed by the then Governor-General to undertake an ethnographic survey to enquire into the conditions of the inhabitants of Bengal and their religion (Buchanan, 1820). Since then anthropologically oriented officers like Risley (1891), Dalton (1872), Grigson (1938), Gurdon (1914), Thurston (1909) and many others, were assigned,in addition to their administrative duties, the task of preparing handbooks, gazetteers, monographs, etc., on the tribes and castes of India. Thus, owing to their efforts, the first set of ethnographic data, collected by these British Officers, for the purpose of colonial administration, was brought to light.

Among the Indian nationals, S.C. Roy, who studied the several tribes of Bihar, brought to light for the first time the devastating effects of contacts on some of the jungle tribes of Bihar. While his opinions are well known about the major tribes in one of his papers, he highlights the evil effects of contacts on the minor tribes in the following words:

"With the opening of the country by roads and railways under the British rule and the gradual deforestation of the country and even the increasing restrictions in the use of forests, those forest tribes (Birhor & the Korwa) are slowly but surely dying out partly from famine and partly from loss of interest in life" (Roy, 1931: 375-77).

The evil effect of culture contacts among the tribals which have had direct bearing on applied anthropological research was taken up by D.N. Mazumdar and A. Aiyappan under the influence of the British functional approach. While Mazumdar studied the Ho and the Korwa tribes of Bihar and reported that they are suffering from imported diseases, loss of ambition in life, great disparity in the proportion of sexes, Aiyappan studied many tribes of South India specially the Irulas, Chenchu, Kadar, etc., and reported about the nature of culture change taking among them.

While the first generation of Indian anthropologists like S.C. Roy, D.N. Mazumdar, A. Aiyappan, N.K. Bose, K.P. Chattopahyay, etc., were engaged in tribal problems in India, there emerged one British-trained missionary, Verrier Elwin, in the horizon of Indian Anthropology, whose idea of establishing a *"National Park"* for the tribals, drew severe criticism. He was called *"isolationist"* and "no changer". However, with certain modifications, when he wrote "A Philosophy for NEFA" (1957), which was considered as the democratically-oriented approach to tribal problems, late Pandit Jawarharlal Nehru, the first Prime Minister of India, wrote a foreword to this volume and appreciated the suggestion proposed by Elwin.

Thereafter, from time to time, many valuable papers on tribal problems, appeared in the anthropological journals like the *Eastern Anthropologists, Man-In-India, Journal of Social Research,* etc. Among these Journals, one issue of the Eastern Anthropologist of 1949 and two issues of J.S.R., (1959, 60) deserve specail mention, as they are the special numbers on tribal problems as well as Action and Applied Anthropology.

Books by Sachchidanand (1964), Vidyarthi (1963, 78, 80), Naik (1957), Biswas (1956), Das and Raha (1963), Fuchs (1960), Roy-Burman (1964), Mathur (1977) contain valuable materials on the tribal problems in India. The introduction of the Community Development Programmes in Rural India, after the independence, has not only stimulated village studies from theoretical and methodological points of view, but also encouraged a number of researches from applied angles. In this context the publications of S.C. Dube (1958), S.K. Dey (1964), Henry Orenstein (1963s), Oscar Lewis (1954), etc., have provided a strong base for the theory and methods of applied anthropology in India. Of late, Budhadeb Chaudhari has edited (1982) a volume—"Tribal Development in India: Problems and Prospects", which is considered to be the best piece of monograph and the latest one, in the field of tribal development and applied anthropology in India.

Among the major areas of applied anthropology, discussed in these volumes, special mention may be made of the following:

1. Education and Culture.
2. Health and Culture.
3. Family Planning Programmes.
4. Applied aspects of Physical and Medical Anthropology.
5. Problems of Crimes and the Criminals.
6. Community Development Programmes.
7. Industrial and Urban Problems.
8. Problem of culture contacts.
9. Labour Problem.
10. Other Socio-Economic Problems.
11. Problems of National integration; etc.

Thus, in Indian anthropology the researches on applied anthropology have gone ahead, which have not only helped the Govt., at different levels, but have also provided a set of concepts, theories and methods at the academic level.

Chapter II

Concepts of Society and Culture

In social anthropology, we usually study the various comparative components of social system, their structure, their organisation, function, etc. The social systems are the interdependent activities, institutions, and values by which people live and it is the job of social anthropologists to identify these components of social systems. Various theories and concepts have been developed of social anthropology to the trichotomatic viewpoints, viz., of the social structure, the social organisation and the social function and here I explain, in brief, some of them, and their interpretations.

Social Structure

The total pattern of social organisation within a culture serves to maintain orderly relationships among individuals and groups, to regulate the production and distribution of wealth, and to provide a setting for the breeding and socialisation of new members of the society. The elements of social structures, therefore, include, among others, the patterns of kinship, descent, and affiliation, the techno-economic system and the politico-legal system. There is considerable debate among anthropologists, however, as to whether social structure is a concrete entity consisting of observable social facts or whether the concept refers merely to the principles according to which these serial facts are organised.

This point becomes very clear from the various definitions of *social structure,* given by different sociologists and social anthropologists.

The most catholic definition of *social structure* has been given by the *Notes and Queries on Anthropology* (Sixth Edition; 1951) where it is said "By the social structure is meant the whole network of social relations in which are involved the members of a given community at a particular time. It defines, on the one hand, the forms in which people are grouped for social purposes in the society, and on the other, the socially recognized ties reflected in the behaviour of individuals to one another and to their social groups" (ibid, p.63).

A.R. Racliffe Brown (1881-1955), the champion of the Structural School of thought, pointed out that "the components of Social Structure are human beings; the Structure itself being an arrangement of persons in relationships institutionally defined and regulated" (1952).

E.E. Evans-Pritchard, while writing on Nuer (1940) restricts "Social Structure to the interrelations of groups, explicitly excluding inter-personal relations".

Fred Eggan (1950) finds the components or Units of social structure in the inter-personal relations which "becomes part of the social structure in the form of status positions occupied by individuals".

E.R. Leach (1954) suggested that "Social Structure (insofar as personal situations are concerned), consists of a set of ideas about the distribution of power between persons or groups of persons".

Levi-Strauss, the most outstanding French anthropologist, holds[1] (1953) that "Social Structure can by no means be reduced to the ensemble of social relations to be described in a given community".

M. Fortes (1949) while writing about the kinship of Tallensi, says that:

"........the elements of social structure are the constant features in the pattern of organisation of all activities in which the relation is significant".[2]

According to S.F. Nadel (1957) "Structure is a property of empirical data of objects, events or series of events—something they exhibit or prove to possess on observation or analysis; and the data are said to exhibit structure in as much as they exhibit a definable articulation, an ordered arrangement of parts. Nadel further argues that "structure indicates an ordered arrangement of parts which can be treated transposable, being relatively invariant, while the other parts themselves are variable."

In addition to these definitions of social structure, as given and analysed by the distinguished social anthropologists, I now give below some pointed definition of social structures as given by some eminent sociologists with a view to throw light as to how this concept has acquired an important position among the schools of thought of two sister-disciplines.

Among the sociological works, where the term *social structure* appeared, special mention may be made of Herbert Spencer's (1820-1903) *"Principles of Sociology"* (1885; vol. I) and Emile Durkheim's (1858-1917) *Divisions of Labour* (1893), but the latter sociologists gave a pointed definition of Social Structure, some of which are quoted below:

K. Mannheim, in his book *Ideology and Utopia* (1936) defined social structure as "Social Structure is the web of interacting social forces from which have arisen the various modes of observing and thinking....."

M.Ginsberg, in his book *"Reasons and Unreason in Sociology"* (1947) writes that: "Social Structure is concerned with the principal forms of social organisation, i.e., types of groups, associations and institution and the complex of these, which constitutes societies...a full account of Social Structure would involve a review of the whole field of comparative institutions". R.M. MacIver and C.H. Page, in their book—*Society* (1950) define social structure as:

"....all the various modes of groupings....together comprise the complex pattern of social structure....in the analysis of the social structure the roles of the diverse attitudes and interests of social being is revealed".

From the perusal of above definitions, as given by both the sociologists and social anthropologists, it appears that the theory of social structure has attracted the attention of social scientists and therefore, in social anthropology, which is also called as "Primitive Sociology", Social Structure is empirical reality. It is dealt with by description, by analysis and by comparative studies in social anthropology.[3]

Social Structure: A Model?

The term "model" is used variously. Ackoff (1962:III) makes a distinction between a model of a class of phenomena and a model of a problem situation. Both are mathematical models.

Levi-Strauss[4] (1963:277) argues that *Social Structure* refers to a group of problems of wide scope. Again, for him social structure is concerned with the models built up after the empirical reality rather than with the reality itself (p. 279). Further, social structure does not have its own field among social studies. "It is rather a method to be applied to any kind of social studies" (ibid).

Levi-Strauss, thus, gave a plausible explanation of Social Structure, as mentioned above. But it is not clear how social structure will be a group of problems, a model and also a method. And Gopala Saran[5] (1983) is right when he says that "it is none of these. It is a concept, an analytical tool, which the anthropologist was to describe, arrange, and organise his empirical data" (p. 99).

Saran further says that a model, no doubt, has a structure, but the way term "social structure" is used in anthropology, it cannot be called a model (ibid).

Social Organisation

The term "Social Organisation" is often used as synonym for social structure. Raymond Firth (1951) distinguished between the two terms: while both structure and organisation are aspects of every social system, structure is essentially the static and organisation, the dynamic aspect. Structure consists of ideals and expectations and provides members of the society with a reliable guide to action (statuses and roles). "Social Organisation" refers to the systematic ordering of social relations by acts of choice and decision; these acts are guided by precedence that are provided by the social structure and limited by the range of possible alternatives. Thus, observable behaviour including change and variation in a social system is accounted for in its social organisation. Specifically, the acts of individuals responding to influences from inside or outside (for Forth, mostly the former) their social systems, lead to fundamental changes in the values, norms, ideals and expectations of the society. Further more, as the term implies, social organisation involves unified, planned, and concerted efforts or actions—i.e., groups of individuals co-operating a period of time.

Human social organisation is a process that brings about the ordering of social activities as a result of ongoing decisions—making by the members of a society. The bi-sexual nature of a human species, as well as the long period of dependence of human offspring necessitates the development of an orderly social life. While human beings are not the only social animals, they are also the people whose social life pervasively depends on share, learned cultural tradition.

It is an attempt to conceptualize and analyse the regularity of social activities exhibited by members of various societies that the concept of social organisation as well as the related social structure and function have been developed.

Radcliffe Brown says that while social structure refers to an arrangement of persons, social organisation[6] refers to an arrangement of activities. Social organisation, according to Radcliffe Brown, is the arrangement of activities of two or more persons, which are adjusted to give a unified combined activities. An example is the organisation of work in a factory. The manager, the foreman and other workers, etc., have certain tasks to perform as a part of total activities.

Thus, while social structure, as discussed earlier, is an arrangement of persons in institutionalised roles and relationship, social organisation is the study of arrangement of activities of human beings of a given society at a specific time and period. Social structure and social organisation are, as a matter of fact, the two sides of the same coin.

Social organisation, stucture and function stem from the attempt to view human social life as an ordered system. Raymond Firth, whose thinking is reflected clearly, distinguishes these three interrelated concepts. The structure aspect of social relations are the principles or rules on which their form depends. An example of structural principles is the set of rules which under-line the kinship system such as matrilineal or patrilineal descent, which gives a continuity of form to social system. The functional aspect of social relations are the ways in which they serve given ends, either individual or collective. Thus, the social system has been conceptualised as an orderly purposive and stable system; its purposiveness is conceptualised in terms of structure. But social systems are also dynamic: People adopt different strategies to secure their ends, people succeed one another in desired position groups contained with one another. Moreover, while the principles of a social structure may limit, the range of social activities, quite often alternative exists. This dynamic situationally determined choice-based social activities is conceptualised in terms of social organisation. The organisational aspect of social activities is then the directional activities which maintains forms and serves ends. Social Organisation, in this way, is the systematic ordering of social relations by acts of choice and decisions. The study of social organisation, in that way, focusses on the individual actor's evaluation of a situation and the choice among alternative courses of action and is particularly helpful for the study of social change. In this way, it may be concluded that the concept of social organisation emphasises the arrangement of activities and variations. It is further said that the study of social organisation is closer to the empirical facts and more concrete than the study of social structure. As much, it provides a needed complement to structural analysis. While analysis of social structure utilizes "Mechnical models" (Levi-Strauss, 1963) describing normative behaviour, the analysis of social organisation should imply "Statistical model" based on actual behaviour.

Community and Society

In social anthropology and sociology the study of community is very important. It is said that the community is as the pillars of the ancient society. People were divided into different communities and share joint responsibilities. The term "community" is, however, used with much freedom by sociologists to characterise a wide range of groups whose members share a sense of identity, specific interest, values and a role of definitions with respect to others.

A corporate community is itself a small cultural system and members of a community derive their personal identity from their community membership. Communities have their distinct territorial boundries. These physical boundries express their social boundedness as well. In such a community the people share a common economic resource base. Equality of wealth is expected and inequality is viewed with fear and suspicion as a threat to the equilibrium of the community.

Community has been defined by many sociologists, some of which are given below:

According to MacIver and Page (Society): "Whenever the members of any group, small or large, live together in such a way that they share, not this or that particular interest, but the basic condition of a common life, we call that common life a community."

In this definition an emphasis has been given on "basic condition of a common life". Thus, the members of the community must share a common interest for the cause of the society.

According to Ogburn and Nimkoff, "a community may be thought of as a total organisation of social life within a limited area".

C.H. Cooley defines, "a community, on the other hand, is a permanent social group embracing a totality of ends of purposes".

Lindman says, "a community if we define it explicitly, is a consciously organised aggregation of individuals residing in a specified area or locality endowed with limited political autonomy, supporting such primary institutions as schools, churches, etc."

Zinsberg says that "the community may be described as the entire population occupying a certain territory held together by a common system of rules regulating the intercourse of life".

In this way community has been defined by many sociologists who have also suggested certain bases of community which are discussed below:

According to MacIver, "there are two bases of community;"
   (a) Locality (Geographical, linguistic, dress, food habits, etc.),
   (b) Community sentiments (thinking, thought, ideologies, common cause of activities, etc.)

However, there are some other factors which are also counted as the bases of communities which may be listed below:
(a) Common life
(b) Particular Name.
(c) Permanency
(d) Self-dependency
(e) Spontaneous Birth, etc.

In this way various types of bases have been provided by the sociologists for understanding the characteristics of community in sociological perspective.

Society

The term "society", like many other terms used by anthropologists, derives from common usage and consequently is variously defined by different scholars. Nevertheless, all students of anthropology sagree that the term refers to social grouping or collectivities.

Zinsberg says, "a society is a collection of individuals united by certain relation or modes of the behaviour which mark them from others who do not enter into these relations or who differ from them in behaviour."

W. Green has defined the society in the following way. He says, "a society is a largest group to which any individual belongs. A society is made up of a population, organisation, time, place and interest."

According to MacIver, "society is a system of usages and procedures, of authority and mutual aid of many groupings and divisions, of control of human behaviour and of liberties. This everchanging complex system is called society. It is the web of social relationship."

In their attempts to define what kind of social groups may usefully be termed societies, anthropologists generally agree that the central features are relatively large size, relative self-sufficiency, and continuity of existence across generations. Thus a social group which can sustain itself more or less independently, recruits most of its members through socialising (en-culturating) member's children has pattern and predictable inter-generational interaction, is larger than a community and is more generalised than an institution may legitimately be called a society. It should be noted that societies unlike nations do not always have specific political boundaries.

The functional pre-requites of a society have been enumerated by Aberle et al. (1950) in their classic article on the subject. According to him provisions are made to him for adequate relationship to the environment and for sexual recruitment in the society; role differentiation and role assignment; a communication system; shared cognitive orientation; a shared and articulated set of goals; normative regulation of the means used by members to attain socially appropriate goals; regulation of the expression of affect; socialization, mechanism and means for effectively controlling disruptive behaviour.

There are two major orientation towards the study of society. One school often called functionist (or equilibrium-model oriented), views society as fundamentally stable with episodic periods of greater or lesser change. The functionalist typified by Talcott Parsons, analysed society in terms of a homeo-static equilibrium model which suggests that society, like a pendulum, may respond to various influences by swinging in diverse directions but over-time consistently seeks its centre. The other school rooted in Marxist theory, sees change as a social constant generated by the irreconcilable conflicts obtaining between the various groups which constitute a society. These conflicts theorists represented by Mortan Fried, among others, view times of social stasis as temporary brought about by the repressive measures of a society's powerful members who seek to perpetuate their political ascendancy. To date, various efforts to synthesize the two approaches into one general theory of society have not been successful.

Characteristics of Society

There are various characteristics of society and among them special mention may be made of the following:
 (a) Society is a network of relationship.
 (b) It is based on social-interactions
 (c) There is a sense of mutual awareness among the members of the society.

(d) Society exists only there where social beings behave.
(e) Finally, society is a complex form of individuals in which both are interdependent on each other. Without individuals we cannot imagine a society or vice versa.

Difference between community and society:

Community	Society
(A) A community can be identified.	A society cannot be seen.
(B) A community is related to an area.	Society has no territorial limit.
(C) A community commands over things within its area.	In a society things are owned usually by the members of the society.
(D) There is a less chance of co-operation among the members of the community.	In a society co-operation prevails among the members of the society along with conflicts and tensions.

Institutions and Associations

All known human societies have standard ways of doing things which consist of three major components: Norms serving as goals and as guidelines for behaviour, roles constituted by norms, and pattern behaviour attached to the norms and roles. Behaviour, which is standardised in this manner, is called institutionalised behaviour, and the whole system of standardization of a behavioural pattern, is called an institution. These concepts appeared to require that multiplicities of persons be engaged in the standard ways of doing things; that the actions involved be determined by inter-dependents norms linked together and embedded in roles; and that there occur different roles or role sets in complimentary relationships.

There are, however, a number of ambiguities in the use of the term first, not all behaviour patterns are institutions even if they are normatively governed. Secondly, the term is often applied to an association such as the Smithsonian Institutions (Washington D.C.) or an asylum, the usage appearing to refer to chartered organisations. The ambiguity here is that an association is an organisation but doing things by means of associating into organisation is an institution.

Thirdly, many behaviour patterns which seem quite normative are not ordinarily considered institutions. Generally, then, the central notions of institutions involve actions attached to and controlled by the norms entailed in complex role sets applying to multiplicities of persons over extended territory.

Many sociologists have attempted to define institutions in their own ways. For the benefit of the students some of the definitions are quoted below:

W.G. Sumner in his book *Folkways* says, "an institution consists of a concept (like idea, notion, doctrine, etc.) and structure like:

LAW
↓
FOLKWAYS
↓
CUSTOMS
↓
ORTHODOXY
↓
INSTITUTION

According to MacIver and Page, "Institutions are defined as established forms of procedure".

C.H. Cooley defines, "an institution is a complex organisation of collective established in social heritage and meeting some persistent need".

A.W. Green says, "an institution is the organisation of several folkways and more into a unit which serves a number of functions".

According to MacIver, "there are two types of institutions: (a) Associational Institution (like college, school, universities, etc.); and (b) Communal Institution (like fares, festivals, etc.).

As a matter of fact we are born and live in an association but we move and act through institutions.

Many have attempted to classify institutions. Malinowski lists seven institutions which mostly revolves about the basic human biological needs, (for example, the need for getting food, the need for sex, etc.). C. Panunzio lists seven or eight institutions which apparently revolves about basic socio-cultural needs. He does not attempt Malinowski's biological reductionism, which has been almost universally abandoned since diverse social orders and actions can be adapted to each of Malinoswki's postulated need, i.e., there is no casual connection or isomorphy between socio-cultural forms and biological needs. Categories of institutions are useful only if they relate to a theory of human society and culture and specifically a theory of socio-cultural functions.

Associations

This term refers to two domains of social life. Sometimes it specifies the relation, a person has regularly with non-kin and others in terms of some shared goals. More often, it specifies social groups organised to pursue definite ends. Since the first usage can be specified adequately by terms such as relationship, co-operation, and collusion (which are, in any case, more precise), whereas the second usage is not adequately covered by another term, the latter seems more important for social science.

The term, "association", points to the social importance of the fact that a number of persons join (or are made to join) together for a purpose. That is, associations involve (i) a group in the strict sense of the term; (ii) its charter expresses its statement written or unwritten, recruitment and extrusion procedure, group property and the group's explicit aims; (iii) more or less standardised operating procedures such as, meetings; (iv) possibly and executive body all of whom may or may not be members; and (v) action towards ends.

On the basis of these criterias a number of sociologists have given definitions of association, some of which are given below for the benefit of the students.

According to MacIver, "we define an association, then as a group organised for the persuit of an interest or group of interest in common".

Gisbert says, "an association is a group of people united for a specific purpose or a limited number of purpose."

C.H. Cooley says, "a group of social beings related to one another in common organisation with a view to securing a specific end".

Usually, an association is formed to obtain certain specific aim. Co-operation, however, is supermost in the functioning of an association. Associations vary vastly in scale and in its size. Most associations are relatively small and localised within a society; although some may relate to parts of the population spread across its entire territory and through many of its segments.

Associations satisfy human needs and wants by creating special organization when other organisation such as families cannot do the tasks required. Associations are extra-ordinarily adaptable modes of social organisation in part because most of them can be readily extinguished when no longer in use. They are very rare in simple societies.

It is finally concluded that an association has a charter of laws for the guidance of its members. An association is a concrete reality in terms of Levi-Strauss. It is not permanent and the membership is always optional.

Difference between Association and Community
Social Group

Association	Community
Association is formed	- Community is born automatically.
It is formed achieving specific ends and aims.	- It is formed to protect the whole human life.
Membership is optional.	- Membership is compulsory.
Association is temporary.	- Membership is permanent.
Structure is smaller than the community.	- Structure of a community is always larger than the association.
Not related to any particular area.	- Always associated with the area.

A social group is a kind of social organisation, in contrast to social network, aggregations and classes. Social groups are generally small organisations composed of individual tied together in personal relation.

Gillin and Gillin say, "a social group, thus, grows out of and requires a situation which permits meaningful response between the individuals involved, common focussing of attention on common stimuli and interest and the development of certain common drives, motivation or emotions".

According to Bogardus, "a social group may be thought of as a number of persons, two or more, who have some common objects of attention, who are stimulating to each other, who have a common loyality and participate in similar activities".

Types of Groups

According to Ward and Giddings, "There are two types of social groups: (a) *Voluntary group* (party, club, etc.), and (b) *Non-voluntary group* (family or clan, country, etc.)"

According to Schumner, 'There are two groups viz. (a) *In-Group*, and (b) *Out-Group*". According to Schumner, in an *In-group*, there is a we-feeling as we find in a family, whereas in an *Out-Group* (such as political party, etc), we find lack of such we-feeling.

Miller says that social groups may be divided into two broad categories viz. (a) Vertical (b) Horizontal Group. According to Miller modern society represents vertical group while ancient society represented the Horizontal groups.

Edward Ross is of opinion that social group may be divided into three broad categories:
 (i) Local Group
 (ii) Likeness Group, and
 (iii) Interest Group.

However, the most important classification of social group was given by C.H. Cooley. He says that in a Primary group persons have face to face relation. The best example of Primary group is the family or kins. However, in a secondary group relations are based on mutual interest, such as, the friends, trade union, etc.

Band and Tribe

The band is the simplest level of social organisation and it is marked by very little political organisation. It consists of small group of families. Cohesion comes through charismatic leadership, marriage alliances with members of other bands and family organisations. As a matter of fact, band is deeply associated with the nomadic section of a tribal group. In India as well as in Africa some of the tribes are divided into a number of bands who move for the search of food gatherings and hunting in a small group, which is called as band.
Tribe

Although this term is widely used in a reference to the preliterate people in many parts of the world, there is no commonly accepted definition of the word.

Originally, a tribe is defined as a social group having a simple technology, primitive economy, prevalence of animistic and homogeneity of culture. On the basis of these characteristics, usually an ethnic group is defined as a tribe.

Social Norms and Social values

In one sense, a norm is simply a shared standard of a social group to which members are expected to conform. In another sense, norm may mean the model or average social behaviour, attitude or opinion found in a social group. Homan (1950) defines, "norm" as an idea in the minds of members of a group, an idea that can be put in the form of a statement specifying what the members of other group should do or ought to do, or are expected to do under given circumstances. These norms are not the same as what is actually done in a given situation or even what members of the group believe, is done. These are simply standard to which people are expected to conform probably because they are believed beneficial for the group. Sherif and Sherif (1948) suggest that there is a process of norm formation. Faced with an ambigous situation, a group of individual initially will have widely divergent opinions, but then the opinions gradually converge, thus giving rise to normative behaviour.

Social Values

As a matter of fact this term refers to the quality of object, material or non-material, which makes it more or less, desirable than other objects. However, in sociological perspective social values mean all those personal relations which exist in a society, must have a sense of bearing on the members of the society in a larger perspective. Again, a relationship with another human being may have economic value, if it enhances the satisfaction of ones physical and emotional needs. A more rigorous interpretation would restrict attachment of economic value to material objects.

In connection with the study of social values we usually

come across the term, *"Value Heirarchy"*. A value heirarchy is a model for ranking cultural values; ideally, such a model should be crossed culturally valid. Values are essentially the meanings attached to categories of experience and as such culturally relative. The relationships between categories— Taxonamic or part-whole are also culturally approved. Nevertheless, anthropologists have proposed cross-culturally valid value heirarchies. One model contains (a) value premises at the top of the heirarchy which defines the nature of humanity and society; (b) then, focal values which specify areas of central importance; (c) then, directives or rules of behaviour, and (d) finally, valued activities, situations or objectives already existing in the society. In this way besides sociologists, social anthropologists have also attempted to undertake the study of social norms and social values in both a primitive and complex societies.

Culture and Civilization

The word, "Culture" has a very broad meaning in anthropology. Various definitions and interpretations have already been given in the first chapter. However, some of the definitions are again given here for the benefit of the students and relevance of the subjects here.

For the first time an anthropological definition of culture was given by E.B. Tylor (1832-1917), in his famous books *Primitive Culture* (1871) which runs as, "Culture or civilization taken in its wide ethnographic sense, is that complex whole which includes knowledge, belief, art, morals, law, custom and any other capabilities and habits acquired by man as a member of the society".

According to Malinowski, "Culture is an instumental reality, an apparatus for the satisfaction of the biological and derived need" (1944). Malinowski, emphasised on the biological aspect of culture and explains the biological characteristics of human behaviour. Although he made a distinction between "need" and "impulses" and emphasised on the satisfaction need which leads to a number of functions. Malinowski's interpretation of culture provoked his great competitor and a rising star in the British anthropology, A.R. Radcliffe Brown (1881-1955), who totally disagreed with Malinowski in the biological interpretation of culture. Radcliffe did not agree with the use of the world, "Culture" in studying social institutions but his analysis of "Social Structure" amounts to wider perspective of culture, as it appears from the contents and things of the subject dealt with in the social structure.

While the British anthropologists were making different interpretations of culture and emphasised more on the integral and psychological aspects of culture, which helped them to develop various meanings and interpretations of culture (Ruth Benedict, 1934; Linton, 1945; Mead, 1928, etc.), which led to the development of "Pattern" and "Culture and Personality" school of thought.

David Bidney (1953), a famous theoretician of the Indiana University (U.S.A.), pointed out that four facts, viz., the artifacts, socio-facts, agro-facts and menti-facts should be considered as the characteristics of culture. In this connection David Bidney (ibid) also pointed out that no sharp line of demarcation can be drawn between the sphere of culture, on one hand, and that of the organic and psychological phenomena, on the other. Bidney defines, "Culture is an attribute of human behaviour and is, therefore, to be studied as an integral part of human behaviour, not as if it were a dynamic entity capable of acting and developing apart from the organism which express themselves through it". (ibid).

Although the main thesis of Margaret Mead was the study of culture in terms of "personality structure", but the latter researches carried out by her as well as by her associates suggested that the "individuals" achieve some kind of "patterned integration" and, thus, culture becomes part of the individual. According to them "a culture may be said to be just as much the expression, their mode of human psychodynamic adjustment, as it is a condititon for the grooming of successive generations of individuals in this mode" (1952).

A.L. Kroeber though not associated with any school of thought directly, remains an unquestioned chief of American anthropologist for nearly two decades. He put forward his experienced views that anthropology alone was to deal with culture, as such both through total description and through conceptualization or theoretically (1948). He also explained how the study of culture is made at different levels, which gives birth to different branches of anthropology to study culture at different levels and from different angles. According to him, associated with the understandings of culture are knowledge of its past, which gives birth to the study of prehistoric culture; of the most autonomous spatial sector of culture, namely, language; which has given birth to the linguistic anthropology; the racial and biological culture of man has given birth to physical anthropology, which all come within the purview of culture in anthropology. Thus, Kroeber presented a round picture of culture as expressed through the study of different branches of anthropology.

Civilization

"Civilization" has been defined by many scholars, some of which are quoted below, in brief, for the benefit of students. Among all the scholars Redfield's definitions of civilization are widely accepted by the students of civilization.

Redfield, first, coined the term, "Great and Little Tradition". After formulating this term, Redfield put forward his explct definitions of a civilization in various ways. First, he defines civilization as "a complex structure of great and little traditions" (1955). This definition in terms of traditions emphasizes culture content together with its historical sources and level of development. The interaction of great and little traditions can be regarded as a part of the social structure of the peasant community in its enlarged context. Redfield further suggested that we are concerned with those persisting an important arrangement of roles and statuses appearing in such corporate groups as "castes and sects" or teachers", "reciters, ritual leaders" of one kind or another, that are concerned with the cultivation and inculcation of the great traditions.

His second definition of civilization emphasized mainly on the "Social structure of the culture, the structure of traditions and their transmissions". Citing examples from different sources, Redfield pointed out that in a compound peasant society there is a certain kind of the persisting social relation, a certain kind of the social structure, viz, the relations between "Chinese scholar and Chinese peasant" which is important in bringing about the communication of great tradition to the peasant or that perhaps without any one's intention, causes the peasant tradition to affect the doctrine of the learned, constitute the social structure of the culture, i.e., the structure of traditions. From this point of view Redfield defines civilization "as an organisation of specialists, kind of role occupiers to one another and to lay people and performing characteristics functions concerned with the transmission of traditions" (Ibid). Redfield clarified his viewpoint regarding the use of the word "social organisation of tradition". He was of the opinion that this word has been used in a reserved sense, particularly in connection with concrete activity at particular times and places. Social organisation is the way that people put together elements of action in such a way as to get done something they want done. Social structure is a persisting general character, a pattern of typical relationship, social organisation is described where we account for the choices and resolution of difficulties and conflicts that actually went on or characteristically go on. Thus, accordingly Redfield used the term the "social organisation of tradition".

In his third definition of civilization, which he proposed along with Milton Singer, emphasis was made on self-axis, that is, in view of a characteristic world view, ethos, temparament, value system, cultural personality, etc. (1955-79). This definition shows the psychological characterisation and interpretation of understanding a civilization.

In addition to these definitions of civilization, Redfield further emphasized that a civilization has both great regional scope and great historic depth. It is a great whole, in space and in time, by virtue of the complexity of the organisation, which maintains and cultivates its traditions and communicates them from the great tradition to the many varied small local societies within it. In this way Redfield's various theoretical interpretations and methodological study of civilization helped to develop "form of thought" appropriate to the wider system, the enlarged contents, of our anthropological researches.

To Toynbee a civilization is delimited as "an intelligible field of historical study" (1947). He suggested that "it is the conceptions and working habits of the historians, the choices amongst events to find the inclusive and influential, the recognition for temporal chains of inter-connected events, of course, the use of book and document, and then the assumed obligation to compare one civilization with another, that led to this kind of definitions" (1955). For delimitation of civilization, he further pointed out that "a civilization is to be delimited from another civilization. The question is as to the broundaries and degrees and kind of relationship between two civilized societies, and the principal classification of civilizations, which he produces, arranges twentyone civilizations according to twelve degrees of greater or lesser relationship to one another" (Ibid).

A.L. Kroeber gives emphasis on "style" (1952), which is a type of characterization in terms of qualities that are abstracted from what must be located on earth and that are not as dependent on chronology as is Toynbee's characterization. Thus, to Kroeber "a civilization constituted to a considerable extent of an assemblage of styles" (ibid) and is "specifically characterized" by these styles.

Whatever a "style" may be as qualities independent of temporal sequence, Redfield did not support Kroeber and he was of the opinion that Kroeber also "characterized civilization through long history and is concerned with styles as they appear, reach climax and decline (1955). Kroeber does not, like Toynbee and Coulborn, seek to show how one civilization grows out of another or how one institutional arrangement, religion, or political form develops from another, as argued by Redfield (ibid). However, Kroeber talked about direction of change in civilization and said that "it is the direction of change in style in civilization" that he finds fundamental (1952). Kroeber has always been concerned with these transformations of styles through time and studied the art styles of ancient South America (Kroeber, 1952). Again, it was Kroeber who suggested that styles have higher or lower "values" in the study of civilization.

Social Change

Social change involves changes in the structure of social relationship—i.e., changes in social role and the relation between them, and changes in the relations between group and institution. Generally, cultural changes are closely related to and may precede or precipitate social changes, but not necessarily show. Thus, sometimes the distinction between social change and cultural change is very crucial. In the narrow sense, cultural change involves alterations in ideas and believes about how things might be done, or values and norms about how things should be done. In contrast, however, social change involves changes in the structure of the social relationship.

Whether the change is externally or internally induced, whether it is deliberately planned or not and whether or not it involves social and cultural elements, many of the processes are similar. The basis for all changes in socio-cultural system lies in the variation in ideas, values of how small a society, how simple its culture, and how strict and disciplined its socialization pattern, the life experiences of each individual are unique.

This salient fact is too often obscured by the theories and concepts of social scientists which ignore individual variation and which stress the duplication and replication of uniformity (e.g., shared norms.).

Yet without differences between individuals and without a capacity to conceive new ideas, no society capable to conceive new ideas, no society could long endure. The basic fact of cultural system is dynamic change adaptations to altered circumstances of life. The most important kind of variation between individuals in this respect is differences in their cognitive maps of the social and physical world they live in, as well as differences in the ways they adjust to their world. Thus all human individuals are potential sources of new ideas about social relationships as well as new ideas of cultural things and ways. Such permutations and recombinations of older cultural ways into new configuration are called innovations. Once conceived, innovative ideas have to be communicated (or diffused) and accepted by others before they become new elements of a social pattern. Those, which initially tried, may be later discarded. Those which are retained may become radically transformed as they are fitted into existing social pattern.

In the study of cultural and social change, the work of Malinowski—the *Dynamics of Culture Change* (1945) is an excellent work which provides a good theoretical interpretation of the study of changes specially in the Tribal societies of the world.

CHAPTER III

Marriage and Family in Primitive Societies

Concepts

Marriage may be defined as a publicly recognised and culturally sanctioned union between a male and female. Which is intended to be enduring, to give primary (but not necessarily exclusive) sexual rights in each other to the couple, and to fulfil further social functions. Definitions of marriage that depend on a specific social function such as the legitimation of children cannot hold universally, because for any given function at least a few societies can be found that do not include it in marriage. On the other hand, a limited number of ends, including child rearing, economic partnership between husband and wife, and the formation of alliances between kin groups, are characteristic of marriage in many societies.

The words *male* and *female* refer here not to physical gender so much as the socially assigned sex role each partner takes in marriage—a qualification necessary, because a few societies allow someone to marry a member of his or her own sex or even a ghost or spirit. To make the definition fit other rare forms of marriage, "male" and "female" would also have to include several people of one sex acting as an individual. Probably no definition, however, is stretched and qualified, which can encompass all societies and all the relationships that have been called marriage.

Definitions

A number of anthropologists have struggled to formulate a definition of marriage that would apply to all human societies. These anthropological definitions may be classified into two categories. The early definitions of marriage that have been formulated prior to 1955 and the modern definitions that have been proposed after 1955.

The early definitions of marriage throw light on various criterias that are required to constitute a marriage. The definitions of marriage offered by the 19th century evolutionists emphasised that marriage is a ritually recognised union between a man and a woman, that the spouses live together and that the couple have clearly recognised mutual sexual rights (Westermarck, 1929). This definition cannot be applied to all societies because there are some societies which contract marriages without a ritual ceremony, there are some societies in which the couple do not live under the same roof and there are several societies in which the spouses are permitted to have extra-marital relations.

Almost similar definitions of marriage were offered by anthropologists in the first half of the present century. Murdock defines marriage as a universal institution that involves residential, co-habitation, economic co-operation and formation of the nuclear family. This definition also cannot be applied to all human societies because there are some societies like the Nayar of Kerala where husband and wife live separately, do not have economic co-operation and do not form the basis of the nuclear family.

Different definitions given by other anthropologists say that marriage "is a union between a man and the woman, such that children born to the women are the recognised legitimate off spring of both parents" (Seligman). This definition is also not satisfactory. If we accept this definition, the union of a man with several women or of a woman with several men cannot in strict sense be called marriage. There are some societies like Nuer in which "woman marriages" takes place between individuals of the same sex. In the "woman marriage" of Nuer, a woman who lost her husband without a male issue, assumes the role of her late husband and marriages a woman and procures the services of a male kin, man or friend to beget children through her. The children so begotten are treated as a children begotten by a widow's deceased husband. Nuer "woman marriage" is not a union between a man and the woman, hence it cannot be regarded as marriage according to the definition of marriage given above. Therefore, anthropologists have been of the view that it has been difficult to arrive at a common definition that will satisfy the patterns of marriage in all human societies.

Modern Definition

During the last three decades the definition of marriage has undergone a great deal of re-thinking. Many anthropologists tried to define marriage in such a way that it holds good to all human societies. Kathleen Gough, for instance, defines marriage as "a relationship established between a woman and one or more other persons, which provides that a child born to the woman under circumstances not prohibited by the rules of the relationship, is accorded full birth-status rights common to normal members of his society or social stratum". This definition does not cover some of the societies like the "Azande of Sudan" which allow a form of marriage based on homosexuality.

William N. Stephens defines marriage as "a socially legitimate sexual union, begun with public pronouncement, undertaken with the idea of permanence, assumed with more or less explicit marriage contract which spells out reciprocal economic obligations between spouses, and their future children". This definition also falls short of many facts occurring in several human societies. Most societies do have taboo periods during which intercourse between couples is not permitted. In many societies extra-marital sex is allowed. In some societies where high divorce rate exists, the idea of permanent relationship between woman and her husband does not exist. In a few societies the union of a man and a woman does not involve any marriage contract. Thus, the definition proposed by William N. Stephens is hard to match against all human societies. It is difficult to arrive at a definition of marriage that will satisfy all situations in all societies.

Characteristics of Marriage

Charter: One of the characteristics of marriage is its charter. The charter of marriage explains why marriage exists and what are the objectives of marriage. The charter of marriage differs from one society to another. Some societies say that institution of marriage has come into existence because of God's creation. Some societies attribute it to the genius of their ancestors. Thus, different societies explain why the institution of marriage exists. The objectives of marriages, defined by the charter of marriage, are also different in different societies. According to some societies, the primary objective of marriage is to create an intimate relationship between man and woman. Some societies say that the objectives of marriage are to procreate children and to perpetuate the family life. Some other societies like the Chukchi of Siberia say that a man needs a woman to dress the meat and skins of the game he kills, to cook food and to make clothing and, therefore, a man and a woman are united through marriage. The Eskimo men from Baffinland, a Canadian Island in the Arctic Ocean, marry because women have to do rowing in the same boats while men have to steer the boat. With these exceptions everywhere, incest was or is prohibited. Incest tabu or incest taboo refers to the prohibition against sexual union and marriage between blood relatives namely parents and children, brothers and sisters. Leaving aside the ancient Egyptian Inca and Hawallan royal families, incest taboos are almost universal. What is the origin of incest taboos? Why incest taboos are almost universal? etc. Anthropologists have proposed different theories regarding the origin and universality of incest taboos.

(i) Edward Westermarck explained that primitive people recognized that mating of close kin produces bad results such as abnormal, or insufficient number of children and, therefore, incest taboos were created.

(ii) R.H. Lowie proposed that human beings everywhere have innate instincts to avoid incest, hence incest taboos arose.

(iii) Edward Westermarck further argued that people who have been brought up together since earliest childhood such as brothers and sisters, would not be sexually attracted to each other, hence incest taboos came into existence.

(iv) Sigmund Freud asserted that children acquire an unconscious desire for the parent of opposite sex, and that incest taboo serves as a device to repress such desires and save the family.

(v) Edward Burnett Tylor stressed that early people married members of other families, promoted co-operation among families, enlarged the size of group from which they could choose mates and helped themselves to survive and, thus, the incest taboo arose because it provided a survival advantage.

(vi) Bronislaw Malinowski stated that sexual competition among family members would create so much rivalry and tension that the family could not function as an effective unit and that since the family must function effectively for society to survive, society has to curtail competition within family and that the incest taboo is imposed to avoid conflict within and disruption of the family.

(vii) Kinsly Davis emphasised that incest taboos are universally practised because they prevent role confusion within the nuclear family in all human societies.

(viii) George Peter Murdock rejected the theories of Westermarck and Lowie but accepted the theory of Freud to some extent and proposed his own theory which states that enculturation, and several other factors and forces are responsible for the origin and universality of incest taboos.

(ix) Marian Slater suggested that the demographic attributes or early human populations were responsible for the origin of incest taboo. Once the incest taboo was created it continued to this day. The average life span of an individual was between 25 and 35 years. If the life span was from 25 to 35 years and if puberty started from 13 to 16, there was not much likelihood of a boy having sexual relations with his mother. If a woman had five children and lived until she reached 35 years, only the oldest male child who lived to maturity could become the father of one of her children, the last one. So, inbreeding became relatively difficult and people had to seek mates outside the family if they were going to mate at all. Thus, demographic features like short life span, relatively few offspring surviving to reproductive, maturity, wide spacing of child births, and a random sex ratio rendered intra-familial breeding unlikely and led to the creation of incest taboo which in course of time become a tradition and continued to the present day (Slater).

Apart from the prospective rules in the form of incest taboos, there are rules in the form of endogamy and exogamy. (*exo*=outside, gamy=marriage). Exogamy is a rule that requires selection of spouse from outside one's own kin group or community. Exogamy may take many forms. It may be lineage exogamy, clan exogamy, phratry exogamy, moiety exogamy or village exogamy. That means one has to take a mate outside her lineage, clan, phratry, moiety, or village. Anthropologists have proposed several reasons for practicing exogamy.

(i) Edward Burnett Tylor argued that paleolithic hunting and gathering bands in all probability exchanged woman in order to live at peace with each other. They might have entered into a system of marital exchange between bands. This arrangement was a positive outcome of need for survival. That means, early human populations practised exogamy in order to live at peace with them and exogamy continued as a custom since those early times.

(ii) Herbert Risley proposed that probably they had a desire to have variety in their life. This desire might have influenced human beings to seek marital ties with strangers, unfamiliar and unknown to them. As a result exogamy had come into existence (Majumdar and Madan).

(iii) Edward Westermarck asserted that children in the same village may not have sexual attraction for each other. Familiarity breeds contempt. Such an aversion for the familiar may be responsible for the origin and continuity of exogamy.

(iv) Audrey Richards argued that in hunting and food gathering societies food is difficult to obtain and women and children become a burden to such societies. To relieve themselves from this burden, societies eliminate females by killing them young. This leads to female infanticide. Female infanticide leads to scarcity of women, which influences the societies to get women from other societies. The best way to get women from other societies is to fight with other societies and capture women from those societies and marry them. This resulted in bride capture. Many tribal societies have proverbs saying "we marry those we fight out", "We marry our enemies". Those proverbs reveal the custom of bride capture. Thus, food scarcity is probably responsible for the origin of exogamy (Richards, 1939).

(v) Several anthropologists argue that exogamy is more associated with unlineal descent groups like lineages, clan, phratry and moiety and since the members of various descent groups believe that they are related through blood, marriage is forbidden within the descent group and hence exogamy arose.

FUNCTIONS OF MARRIAGE

Biological Functions

Like most species of animals, human beings must mate in order to reproduce themselves. However, unlike other animals, human beings tend to form relatively permanent mating pairs. By it self mating does not constitute marriage. Every human society has formulated certain rules and regulations to define a formal, permanent mating relationship as marriage. Partners in a marriage have sexual rights in one another. Through marriage society organizes sex activities. In other words, the institution of marriage regulates and socially validates relatively long-term, legitimate sexual relations between males and females. Marriage serves as a means for getting together to satisfy sex needs and to start the reproductive process. It is through reproduction, human species is replicated and society is perpetuated. Therefore, the institution of marriage serves biological functions.

Economic Functions

As long as discrimination of labour by sex exists, every society has to have some mechanism by which men and women share the produce of their labour. Marriage would be one way to solve this problem. The institution of marriage solves the problem of how to share the work efforts of men and women and how to implement organised division of labour at the individual and inter-personal level. Without co-operation in food getting and obtaining other necessities such as water and shelter, an individual cannot survive. Thus, the institution of marriage performs economic function in the form of bringing economic co-operation between men and women and ensuring the survival of individuals in every society.

Social Functions

Marriage is based on the desire to perpetuate one's family line. It is also a way to acquire new kinsmen, for at marriage one adds not only a spouse but most of a spouse's relatives to one's own group of kin. That means the institution of marriage brings with it, the creation and perpetuation of the family, the formation of person to person relations and linking of one kin group to another kin group. Thus, the institution of marriage serves several functions.

Educational Functions

The care and protection of offspring are at the heart of human social organization. Human infants have the longest period of infant dependency of any primate. The child's prolonged dependence generally places the greatest burden on parent. Unless the parent educate their young through enculturation process, the young cannot acquire culture and carry out bio-social activities successfully. It is the institutions of marriage that entrusts the task of educating the young to the parents and passing on culture from one generation to another. Without education or encluturation process, it cannot serve educative functions for the survival of individuals and for the continuity of culture.

Forms of Marriage

Anthropologists have found that marriage is an universal institution found all over the world and its institutional form has been accepted by all, though it is not the same all over the world. It varies from culture to culture and from society to society. It varies even within a culture and a country, and to some extent within the same people spread over different parts of the country.

However, some of the commonly known forms of marriage all over the world are monogamy, polygyny and polyandry. Among these, however, monogamy is the most popular institution. If one marries a single person at a time, the marrige form is called monogamy. (Greek: *Poly*-multiple; *gamy*-marriage). In other words, the form of marriage depends upon the number of spouses involve in the marriage. The following table shows the various forms and sub-forms of marriage.

Marriage

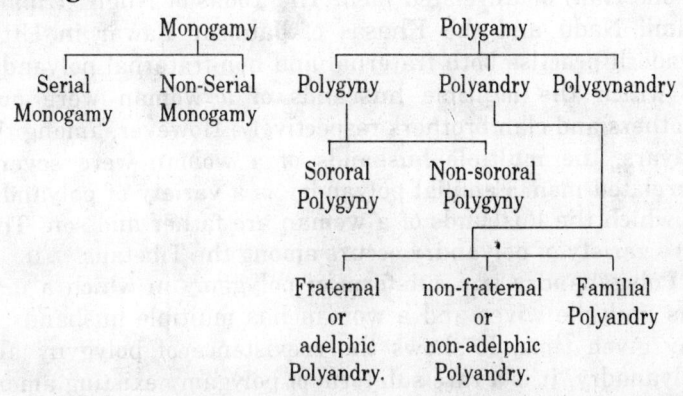

```
                    Marriage
          ┌────────────┴────────────┐
       Monogamy                  Polygamy
       ┌──┴──┐            ┌─────────┼──────────┐
   Serial  Non-Serial  Polygyny  Polyandry  Polygynandry
 Monogamy  Monogamy        │         │
                      ┌────┴────┐    │
                   Sororal  Non-sororal
                   Polygyny  Polygyny
                             │
                    ┌────────┼────────┐
                Fraternal  non-fraternal  Familial
                   or          or        Polyandry
                adelphic    non-adelphic
                Polyandry.   Polyandry.
```

Monogamy is a form of marriage in which an individual has a single wife at any given time. Serial monogamy is a sub-form of monogamy in which an individual has several spouses in succession. The Semangs of Malay forests, for example, limit themselves to one wife at a place. In case of divorce or death of wife, a Semang marries again and again and remains to be monogamous. Non-serial monogamy is a sub-form of monogamy in which an individual has the same single spouse life long.

Polygamy is a form of marriage in which an individual has multiple spouses at any time. Polygamy has many sub-forms: Polygyny and Polygynandry. Polygyny is the sub-form in which an individual has multiple wives at any time. Polygyny exists in two specialized variations: Sororal polygyny and non-sororal polygyny. Sororal polygyny is a variety of polygyny in which the multiple wives of an individual are sisters. Non-sororal polygyny is a variety of polygyny in which the multiple wives of an individual are not sisters.

Polyandry is the sub-form of polygamy in which a woman has multiple husbands at any given time. It appears in three specialized variations: fraternal or adelphic polyandry, non-fraternal or non-adelphic polyandry and familial polyandry. Fraternal or adelphic polyandry is a variety of polyandry in which the multiple husbands of a woman are own brothers (off-spring of the same mother). Non-fraternal or non-adelphic polyandry is a variety of polygandry in which the multiple husbands are either clan brothers (those who belong to one clan) or unrelated men. The Todas of Nilgiri Hills in Tamil Nadu and the Khasas of Jaunsar Bawar in Uttar Pradesh practise both fraternal and non-fraternal polyandry in which the multiple husbands of a woman were own brothers and clan brothers respectively. However, among the Nayars, the multiple husbands of a woman were several unrelated men. Familial polyandry is a variety of polyandry in which the husbands of a woman are father and son. This rare variety of polyandry occurs among the Tibetans.

Polygynandry is a sub-form of polygamy in which a man has multiple wives and a woman has multiple husbands at any given time. It shows the coexistence of polygyny and polyanadry. It is a rare sub-form of polygamy existing among the Todas of Nilgiri Hills, the Khasas of Jaunsar Bawar and the Marquesans of Polynesia. Some men in these societies practise monogamy as well as polyandry. As a result each man will have one wife exclusive to himself and another wife shared along with brothers or clan brothers. That means each man has two wives at any time but at the same time he along with his brothers or clan brothers are multiple husbands to one woman. Therefore, polygyny and polyandry occur simultaneously.

Monogamy

Monogamy occurs in all types of societies in different parts of the world. It occurs among the food gatherers and hunters like the Andamanese, Chenchus and Juang of India, Semang and Sakai of Malaya, Ituri of Congo forests and Arunta of Australia. Several horticultural societies like the Basseri of Iran, Kalmyk of Mongolia, Lapps of Finland and Norway and Dinka of Africa practise monogamy along with polygyny. Likewise numerous agricultural societies like the Dafla, Oraon and Parum of India, Dusun of Borneo and the peasant groups dispersed all over the world practise monogamy and polygyny. Advanced industrialized societies in different parts of the world are monogamous.

Reasons

Why do different societies practise monogamy?

Different societies practise monogamy for demographic, economic, biological, social, legal and psychological reasons.

(i) Monogamy is a response to balanced sex ratio. Even though sex ratio is not uniform, it is approximately 1:1 all over the world. It is commonly said that a man cannot have two wives except by preventing somebody else from having one.

(ii) Monogamy offers a solution to the problem of adapting to the limited availability of various resources in the environment.

(iii) Monogamy favours almost everyone a chance to have at least one spouse.

(iv) Monogamy provides effective sexual gratification for both men and women.

(v) Monogamy keeps intra-sex jealousies and quarrels at minimum.

(vi) Monogamy facilitates relatively easy rules of inheritance, succession and membership in kin groups.

(vii) Monogamy helps to maintain effective child rearing procedures and augment close emotional ties between parents and children.

Besides, these major forms of marriage which have been described above, there are a few sub-form of marriage, viz., the fraternal polyandry, the non-fraternal polyandry, the youth marriage, the levirate, sororate, etc.

In some societies a person may like to marry the sister of his first wife and such a marriage is known as sororate. If the case is just reverse, it is called levirate. Such examples are numerous among the Indian Tribes.

Ways of acquiring a Mate in Tribal Society.

This lession has two objectives. First, it shows the characteristic procedures of mate selection for marital union in different societies of the world. Second, it explains the different forms and sub-forms of marriage and their differential occurrence in various parts of the world and show how differences forms of marriage are solution to certain demographic, biological, economic, social, political and psychological problems existing in different societies.

Ways of acquiring a mate and the forms and sub-forms of acquiring a mate are discussed below.

Acquiring a mate by negotiation.
Acquiring a mate by service.
Acquiring a mate by exchange.
Acquiring a mate by probation.
Acquiring a mate by capture.
Acquiring a mate by intrusion.
Acquiring a mate by trial.
Acquiring a mate by elopment.

The forms and sub-forms of acquiring a mate:

The way of acquiring a mate refers to the characteristic manner in which a spouse is selected. It is the procedure or method of finding or obtaining a wife or husband. To be precise, it may be called the manner of mate choice or spouse selection.

The mate choice or acquiring a mate may be classified into four forms: negotiated mate choice, commonly known as arranged marriage where the consent of the parents is necessary, partial free mate choice where the consent of the parents is necessary, total free mate choice by one or both of the potential spouses, and absolutely free mate choice where the consent of the parents is not necessary.

These three broad forms of choosing a mate appear in several subforms. The negotiated mate choice appears in the form of mate selection by service, by negotiation, by exchange and by probation. The partial free mate choice appears in the form of mate selection by probation. The total free mate choice appears in the form of mate selection, by capture, by intrusion, by trial. The absolutely free mate choice occurs in the form of mate selection by elopment. We will now discuss all these different sub-forms of acquiring a mate in detail.

Acquiring a mate by negotiation

Acquiring a mate by negotiation is quite common to all types of societies. It can be found in simple societies like the Andamanese of Andaman Islands, Chenchus of Andhra Pradesh, Ituri of Congo region in Africa, Siwai of Soloman Islands, and the aboriginals of Australia and in complex societies like the Chinese, Hindus, Japanese, Europeans and Americans (Stephens Bohannian and Middleton).

Obtaining a spouse by negotiations involves long procedures, depending upon the custom, either the boys parents or the girls' parents put forward the proposals and start the negotiations. Go-betweens are frequently used during negotiations. A go-between has more information about a wider network of families than any one family can have. Further more, by using a go-between neither the family of the girl nor the family of the boy loses face if its proposals are rejected by the other party.

Several considerations enter into mate selection by negotiation. Generally speaking, a family or kin group may choose a spouse for its child for any one or more of the following four considerations.

(i) The first consideration is the payment of bride-price, dowry or exchange of gifts. Bride-price payment is a major affair in a vast majority of the societies. Bride-price is also called progeny-price or bride-wealth. It is paid not only in compensation for the woman's loss but also for the loss of the children she will bear. It demonstrates that the marriage is not an individual affair but a group affair because the wealth is received and used by the parents or other relatives of the bride, not by the bride herself. The payment of bride-price grants the groom the right to marry the girl and the right to her children. The bride-price contributes significantly for material eligibility since it may have to be returned if the relationship is dissolved. Bride-price means heavy expenses for the boy's people. For the girl's people it means one of life's main chances for economic gain. With dowry payments the situation is reverse. Dowry means heavy expenses for the bride's people; for the groom's people it means one of life's main chances for economic gain. Gift exchange involves flow of gifts or parents between the groom's people and the bride's people. The bride's people may give gifts or offer dowry to the groom's people and the groom's people may give gifts or offer bride-price to the bride's people.

(ii) A second consideration for acquiring a mate by negotiation is the reputation of the potential spouse's parents and kin group. The reputation may be in terms of social status or it may be in terms of personal qualities that lead to pleasant official ties.

(iii) A third consideration for acquiring a mate by negotiation is perpetuation of marriage arrangement such as those resulting from the obligations of marriage a cross-cousin or a parallel cousin.

(iv) A fourth consideration for acquiring a mate by negotiation is sororate and levirate obligations. According to the levirate or sororate obligations an individual has to choose a widowed sister-in-law or wife's sister as his mate.

After concluding the negotiations on the basis of any one or more of these four considerations, a formal annoucement is made about the acceptance of the proposals, about the amount of bride-price or dowry to be paid or the gift items to be exchanged and about the various procedures to be followed for bringing the boy and the girl together into a marital union at a future date. Thus mate selection by negotiation involves making the proposals and starting and concluding the negotiations on the basis of a number of considerations and an agreement regarding the customary procedures to be followed for uniting the boy and the girl.

Acquiring a mate by service is actually mate selection by

negotiation in which bride-service takes the place of or supplements the bride-price by bride-service. Suiter service refers to the work that the groom does for his bride's family for a variable length of time either before, or during or after marriage is finalized. Mate selection by service occurs in many societies such as the Chuckhee of Siberia, the Kaska Red Indians of Western Canada, the Ojibwa Red Indians of United States, the Sirions Red Indians of Bovia, the Lepchas of Sikkim, the Subanum of Phillipines, the Muria Gond of Bustar, and the many peasant societies in China and India.

Acquiring a mate by exchange

Acquiring a mate by exchange, similar to mate selection by negotiation in which bride-price is substituted by exchange of woman, who are either sisters or female relatives of the grooms. Mate-selection by exchange involves the following considerations:

The first consideration is continuation of inter-family alliances by exchanging daughter or sisters. Exchange of woman is a significant way of establishing a bond between individuals and groups. Quite apart from what is exchanged, the act of exchange itself creates social solidarity.

The second important consideration is obviating the difficulty of paying the bride-price. If there are only a few females or there is a shortage of females in the society woman acquires security value which frequently implies the need for compensation. This difficulty can be overcome by exchanging women between the families.

Mate-choice by exchange occurs in many societies. Among the tribal societies of Australia and Melanesia, families desirous of establishing an alliance exchange females. In these societies a man gives his sister to one who gives in return his sister to the former. Among the Tive of Nigeria women are exchanged between the two families or the kin groups involve in a marriage. In India mate selection by exchange occurs in several tribes like the Muria Gonds and the Baiga of Bustar; the Koya and the Saora of Andhra Pradesh.

Acquiring a mate by probation

Acquiring a mate by probation involves the consent of the girl's parents besides the consent of the girl herself. For example, among the Kukis of Manipur, when a boy is fond of a girl, the girl's parents permit the boy to live with the girl in their house for several weeks and try to understand each other. If the boy and the girl find each other's temperament to be suitable and compatible, the parents of the girl decide to give their daughter in marriage to the boy. If the boy and the girl find each other's temperament to be unsuitable and incompatible, they separate and the boy pays cash compensation to the girl's parents.

Acquiring a mate by capture

Acquiring a mate by capture can be found in many parts of the world. Capture may be physical capture or ceremonial capture. In physical capture a boy adopts a procedure whereby he carries away the girl by force and marries her. In ceremonial capture a boy adopts a procedure whereby he surprises the girl by marking her forehead with a symbol that tantamounts to marriage.

(i) Physical capture takes place in various situations. In one situation a boy may seize a girl from an enemy camp or village, takes her away as a feminine prize and will marry her. Among the Yahomamo of Venezuela and northern Brazil, men of one village abduct women from other villages and take them as their spouses. Among the Nagas of Nagaland and Arunachal Pradesh, there will be raids by one village on another. During such raids men capture women and accept them as wives.

Physical capture may take place in a different situation. A boy who loved a girl but could not get his love reciprocated by the girl ventures to take away the girl by force and marry her. That means the kidnapping takes place without the consent of the girl. This kind of physical capture occurs among the Bagatas and Saoras of Andhra Pradesh, the Ho of Bihar and the Bhils of Rajasthan.

Physical capture may also take place in a still different situation. If a boy and a girl who loved each other but failed to get married, the boy may, with the support of the girl's relatives, take away the girl by force and marry her. That means, the capture takes place with the consent of the girl and with the consent of her relatives. Among the Muria Gonds of Bustar, the capture takes place often at the request of the parents of the girl. Remaining unmarried for too long does not reflect upon her parents, who often request her cross-cousin to take her away. The girl's parents pretend to resist the efforts of the boy when he carries away the girl. The girl also pretends that she is being captured by the would be husband.

(ii) Ceremonial capture is not as complicated as the physical capture. Among the Kharia and the Birhor of Bihar, a man desirous of marrying a girl, whom he cannot acquire by a more straight forward method, would lie in wait for her in a public place or at a fair, and then surprise her by applying vermilion mixed with oil to her forehead. This act of the boy is regarded as equivalent to his marriage with the girl (Majumdar and Madan, 1956).

Why people get a wife by capture? One reason is the security of woman. For example, the Nagas practised female infanticide because of the fear of raids by the enemies. Due to this reason often they had to get a mate from enemy groups. Another reason is that physical capture is cheap and adventuresome, although it is risky too. For example, the Ho have to pay a heavy bride-price if a mate is to be chosen by negotiation. Hence, capturing a woman is considered as the best solution to avoid payment of heavy bride-price. A third reason is the inability of parents to arrange the marriage of their daughters in time. For example, if the Muria Gonds of Bustar do not have the marriage of their daughter in time, they encourage her cross-cousin to take her way.

Acquiring a mate by Intrusion

Acquiring a mate by intrusion can be found only in a small number of societies. In mate selection by capture a boy takes away by force a girl he is fond of but who is unwilling to marry him. On the contrary, in mate selection by intrusion a girl forces a boy to accept her as his spouse. It may occur in the following two situations:

(i) A girl may force a boy she is fond of but who is unwilling to accept her as his mate, to marry her. For example, among the Birhor and Ho of Bihar and, an overfond girl is actually subjected to insulting and harsh treatment, often beaten, turned out and refused food, but she refuses to abandon her intensions, and finally is accepted as one of those impossible girls.

(ii) Mate selection by intrusion may happen if a woman tries to assert herself and secure a rightful status for her, when the man designs to ignore his responsibility. For example, among the Kamars of Madhya Pradesh a woman becoming pregnant in a casual romantic intrigue, intrudes in to the man's house and does not abondon her efforts until she is accepted as the legal wife of the man.

Acquiring a Mate by Trial

Acquiring a mate by trial highlights how a youngman has to prove his qualities of courage and bravery for choosing a mate of his choice. For example, among the Bhils of Rajasthan, during the Holi festival, young men and women dance round a pole or a tree to the top of which a coconut and a piece of jaggary are tied. The women make an inner ring or dancers while the men make an outer ring. The trial of strength begins when a young man attempts to cross from the outer circle of women dancers and reach and climb the pole or tree to eat jaggery and break open the coconut. The women dancers may resist the youngman's efforts by pulling him down, by striking him with broomstics, by tearing at his clothes and hair. If the youngman overcomes the resistance given by the women dancers and succeed's in reaching the top of the pole or tree and eat the jaggery and break open the coconut there, he has the right to select anyone of the women dancers as his mate and take her away immediately.

Acquiring a mate by Elopement

Acquiring a mate by elopement is more or less approved means by which determined individuals can disobey their elders and choose their own mates. Mate selection by elopement occurs among the Fiji of Oceania, Gusli of Kenya, Iban of Borneo, Red Indians and Ojibwa Red Indians of United States, Kaingang Red Indians of Brazil, Kurnai of Australia, Kwoma and Mundugumor of New Guniea, Samoa of Polynesia, Siwai of Solomon Islands, Subanum of Phillipines, Murngin of Australia, Muria Gonds of Bustar, Bagata, Saora, Khond and other tribes of Andhra Pradesh and many other societies. Mate selection by elopement takes place in every known society.

Why should people choose a mate by elopement? When familial or social disapproval blocks a fervently desired marriage, or when a planned marriage, with a distasteful partner is about to be forced on the unwilling one, elopement is a way out.

What is the pattern of elopement? Elopement usually involves "running off", then waiting for some days or months or even one or two years and hoping that the marriage will finally be approved. Generally speaking, the indulgent elders always receive back the over-fond eloped pair and allow them to live as wife and husband.

Rules of marriage

Rules of marriage are very important in the primitive societies, the compliance of which are obligatory for the members of the society. There are many questions such as, when one should marry? where he should marry? whether clan exogamy is practised or not, whether the bride has been brought from within the prohibited degree?, etc; are some of the important anthropological aspects which are discussed in the sub-heading.

Marriage rules are conventionally prescribed by the society; they are expected to be followed in the interests of the solidarity of the group. They are devised so as to provide a system of checks and balances. They often aim at preventing inbreeding and encouraging maximum possible out-breeding within the social norms. Exogamy is the mechanism devised to ensure this. But they also prescribe the limit beyond which one cannot marry; relations with persons outside this prescribed group are strictly forbidden. Endogamy is the principle which decides and fixes up the limits of marriage relations. Endogamy and exogamy do not act across each other; they rather exist simultaneously.

The two main clans of the Toda tribe of South India, the Tartharol and the Teivaliol are essentially endogamous, though their subdivisions, the Sibs are exogamous. The Bhils also have similarly two endogamous groups, the Ujale Bhil and the Bele Bhil. Most of the Indian tribes are endogamous. The cause for their strict endogamy, Majumdar and Madan find (1956) in what they call "the universal fear of the strange, the novel and the unknown".

In many cases, preferences for marriage to a particular kin are only indirectly suggested in a society; they are not rigidly prescribed. A Gond must marry his cousin, but if he has some others choice and wants this prescription to be waived in his favour, a compensation has to be paid to the kin who would be affected by such a concession. When Grigon worked among the Gonds of Bustar he found fiftyfour per cent of Gond marriages to be of this type.

The Kharia and the Oraon marry their cross-cousins. The Khasis of Jaintia Hills in Assam also practice cross-cousin marriage, though with the limitation that a marriage with one's father's sister's daughter cannot be performed so far as one's father is living. The Kadars of Kochin, who are rigidly endogamous, prescribe to their fellowmen a marriage with the paternal cousin.

Cross-cousin marriage is the only form of exogamy under the dual organisation of a society. Cross-cousin marriage is often devised as a balance against the high bride-price, the bargaining of the price is often minimized among the familiar kin. Moreover, the amount lost in paying bride-price for getting a bride is regained in due course when a girl from his family has to be given in marriage to the same family. The simple implication here is that the bride-price paid for A's marriage would be returned to his family, when A's daughter would marry her mother's brother's son. The Gonds of Madhya Pradesh call this form of cross-cousin marriage 'dudhlautawa', i.e., return of milk.

The rules of marriage prescribed, mean that these will be necessarily followed, but that they will be adhered to so rigidly that there will be no exceptions possible would be reading too far a meaning in the proposition. The more a society develops, there are more possibilities of its having some members who would find it difficult to cope with them and who may like to take concessions.

The restrictions of caste endogamy are being now gradually broken in the present Hindu society and a number of inter-caste marriages are now coming in practice. Whereas caste endogamy have certainly been made in the last two or three decades, the barriers of endogamy are also being broken now by the more acculturized tribes like the Bhils, the Gonds and the Santhals, who are trying to get incorporated into the vast body of Hindu castes; they often feel privileged to marry even the lower Hindu castes. This seems a strange influence of Hindu social organization on the tribal peoples coming in their contact. The tribal, when he marries a Hindu caste, has to find his place in the caste hierarchy of the Hindu society.

The prescriptions laid down for marriage do not also warrant those who violate them and will be severally punished. Sometimes they are punished, sometimes they are not; if such punishments have been common in the past, they are now becoming rare. At the most they are possible only in highly isolated and primitive tribes like the Daflas of NEFA. Hammond suggests that the so-called rules concerning marriage and the formation of domestic groups, and other aspects of social organization are best understood as idealized models to which people tend to comform. Allowance for such variance is generally as critical for individual survival and social stability as are the rules themselves. It is often found that marriage rules in most societies, thus, tend to be only explicity stated and compliance with them is often strictly enforced.

Society devises various means to check what it calls inbreeding. Now inbreeding is a relative term as it differs from context to context and from culture to culture. Inbreeding within parents and between siblings has been universally prohibited and hence the rules of incest. The strict implication of the term, "incest" should be understood to mean sex relations between real brothers and sisters. Incest in this sense is known all over the world. Mazumdar and Madan (1956) have pointed out that psychological disorders are the effects and not the cause of incest and do not provide a full motive. The cultural factor of widening the area of co-operative social contact may be considerably responsible for this prohibition on sex-relation between close relatives. Thus, breaches of the rule are often punishable.

Endogamy is also sometimes extended to include village endogamy. However, several tribes of NEFA (now Arunachal Pradesh and other states) marry within village boundaries, but this is possible only when people of the different clans are living in the same village.

Cross-cousin marriages are often the preferred type of marriages in most of the societies of the world. The cross-cousin marriage is of two types. Marriage of a man with his father's sister's daughter, and marriage of a man with his mother's brother's daughter. Of these, the latter type is more popular. This rule, under which one can carry his bilateral kin, is called symmetrical cross-cousin marriage rule by some of the anthropologists.

Cross-cousin marriage falls within the sanction of the society since it is consummated in a clan or kin group other than one's own and is thus essentially exogamous. It is often the preferred type in many societies.

Iravati Karve (1953), who has worked extensively on the kinship organization in India has found that cross-cousin marriage is widely prevalent among the Maharashtrian groups of Hindu societies. She found that in some parts of Maharashtra where cross-cousin marriages have been common, wife's father is often called by the same classificatory term *mama*, which is used for mother's brother. Similarly, among the Maplas of Malabar in South India who allow marriage with all kinds of cousin, the kinship term of address for mother's brother *Mama* is identical with the term for wife's father and husband's father.

Hypergamy and Hypogamy

The concept of hypergamy and hypogamy is typically Indian, in as much as it seems to have been upon caste-structure of the Hindu society. In a large society interactions between different groups become not only easier, but also more marked as they sometimes even cross the usually laid down boundaries. In the Hindu society, right from the days of old scriptures, the prescriptions regarding marrying within one's *gotra* (clan) and marrying within the prescribed *gotras* (clans) had been laid down simultaneously. Apart from other things, the social status was determined by the fact of one's marriage, and a woman's marriage was made a criteria for this. If a woman married a higher-caste family, her own status as well as status of her children subsequently born to her rose higher. If she married a caste lower than her own, not only she and her children suffered an inferior social position, but also a reflection was cast on her own parental family. To prevent a Hindu woman from losing her caste and getting ritual impurity by marrying in a lower caste, Manu (the first law giver) and other ancient Hindu law makers had prescribed hypergamous (*anuloma*) marriage under which a man could marry from within his own caste group, or from those below them, usually a degree only, but a woman could marry only in her own caste group or a caste group above hers. These are called hypergamous marriages. Hypogamous or *pratiloma* marriage, i.e., marriage of a woman from a lower caste was not permitted.

According to these laws, a Brahmin man could marry among Brahmin, Kshatriya anad Vaishya castes; a Kshatriya man among his own and Vaishya castes, and Vaishya with his own and Shudra castes. Likewise, a Vaishya woman could marry a Vaishya, Kshatriya and a Brahmin man; a Kshatriya woman could marry her own caste man and a Brahmin man, and Brahmin woman could marry only a Brahmin man. In spite of these social restrictions, guarded by concepts of ritual impurity and defilement, quite a few examples have been known in the annals of Indian history, thus, showing disregard for the social sanctions. The latest trends of education and enlightenment have broken the rigidities of caste restrictions and relaxations in the form of inter-caste marriages, which have now become possible, but there are still the exceptions, rather than the rule. The caste structure still continues almost in its basic form in most parts of India.

Marriage Payments

Gifts from the husband's kin to the wife's or to the bride's kins are called the bride-wealth or bride-price. In the tribal societies of different parts of the world bride-price is practiced. However, the nature of gifts, in cash or kind vary according to tribe. For example, among the Nuer of America, as reported by Evans-Pritchard, (1940) the bride-wealth includes forty heads (40) of cattle, which are distributed among the different kin groups of the bride. In India, almost all tribes practice bride-price but, as usual, it varies from tribe to tribe. Among the Ollar-Gadba of Korapur (Jha, 1972, 1983), the bride-price is called *Katulugu-Andane*. The villagers of Guga-Guda and Pada-Padar of Ollar villages reported that the bride-price includes at least 10-20 *monos* of rice, one cow with or without a calf, one bullock and one goat or sheep, one *kawdi* of *pendum* (local drink), one sari (Gondei) worth about 15-20 rupees and one rupee in cash. These articles are brought by the groom party in form of bride-price and are handed over to the *Naiko* (the village political head) of the bride's village. The *pendum* (local drink), goat, rice, etc., are meant for feast which is thrown to the villagers or to the kins of the bride's village, while the other articles are given to the bride's mother.

The prevalence of bride-price has also been found among the tribes of Central India like the Munda, Oraon, Ho, Santhals, the Gonds of Bustar, etc., where local drinks of *Mahua* or *haria* is prepared indigenously which is given on the occasion of marriage as bride-price and it is distributed among the villagers of the bride. The bride-price also includes the pieces of saris, cow and calf, some silver ornaments or sometime a few coins, etc. However, among the tribes of Chotanagpur, the nature of bride-price has considerably changed from traditional mode of payment to the modern one. The nature of bride-price is in process of drastic change specially among the tribes of Central India.

Concepts and Definitions of Family

Family is a primary social group, universally recognised to be basis of all human endeavour and activities. The concept of family has been found to exist since time immemorial and at all the levels of cultures. Anthropologists and other social scientists have debated over its origin, functions and other important aspects of this important social institution. It has been, however, believed that it would be impossible to conceive progress of man without a family organisation.

In social sciences, specially in the field of anthropology, Westermarck (1891) was a first scholar to emphasize upon the supremacy of family. His book—*The History of Human marriage* (Ibid), aroused great interest among the scholars and social scientists about the concepts of marriage and family.

William J. Goode, the famous sociologist of America, has given a modern interpretation of family. He points out the differences between family system and the larger social structure. He then proceeds to suggest to universally known characteristics of family and the variables normally associated with the family organisation (1965). The study of family has been getting utmost concern of the modern sociologists and social anthropologists. In the last quarters of the country *"Family Sociology"* has become almost an independent discipline in America and some other European country. Carle C. Zimmerman, one of the chief exponents of the *family sociology* of our times remarks in his paper on the "Family" (1964), "The modern family has moved slowly towards conception of nominalist relations between the other culture and the inner organisation. This movement reached an extreme peak between World Wars I and II. Then the family began a slow turning movement towards a realist relation with the new culture of the Atomic Age."

All these studies provide us an idea about the growing as well as the changing concept of the family.

The family is characterised by some form of institutionalised sex relations, called marriage. As soon as marriage is consumated, it forms another kind of relationship, that of reckoning descent by having same system of nomenclature. It also distinguishes two kinds of kin relationship, agnatic or consanguital, i.e., blood relation and affinal or relationship through marriage. Besides, a family is an economic unit, particularly as far as the mother and infants are concerned. Then there is a division of labour in the family on which sociologists and social anthropologists since the days of Durkheim (1893), have been discussing. Finally, a family necessitates, a common habitation for all its members, where they may live, cook, eat and sleep together.

The famous sociologist MacIver has elaborately explained some of the distinctive features in the family which may be noted below for the benefit of the student:

(a) Universality

Family is found all over the world and in all cultures and civilization. Modern civilization has made tremendous progress but it has not been able to provide a complete substitute of the family. However, there have been variations in the structure and functions of the family throughout the ages.

(b) Emotional Base

Family is an institutionalized emotional behaviour of man and woman. A family integrates together its members in the best possible manner. Affection towards each other, mutual trust and blood ties are the integrative bonds of the family.

(c) Family as an Educational Institution

Family is an institution of informal education or what is called as "Enculturation" of a child. The child learns his first lesson of love, affection, respect, culture and custom in the lap of his mother.

(d) Limitations of Family

The clan, lineage or the sib, which are large in size and extending in character, the family is specifically limited in size. The nuclear family of the modern days particularly in the industralized and urbanized societies, it is becoming more limited in its form and functions.

(e) Social Regulations

Society and family members are interdependent. Society keeps an eye over the members of family by different ways and means. Thus, it expects a number of social obligations from the individual. Therefore, the members of a family are guided by certain customary laws to discharge such social regulations and obligations prevailing in the societies.

In this way, society devises means and mechanisms, to

keep the solidarity of the family intact.

Definition of family

Like the definitions of marriage those of family can also be classified into early ones that have been formulated prior to 1955 and modern ones, which have been formulated after 1955.

Among the early anthropological definitions of the family, those offered by the 19th century evolutionists emphasized that the family was a group based on marriage, common residence, emotional bonds, and stipulation of domestic services. At the same time while some definitions emphasized that the family was unknown among the simplest human society in the Mesolithic and the early Neolithic periods, others concluded that the family was known even to the earliest and rudest human societies.

Like the nineteenth century anthropologists, those in the first half of the twentieth century, have also tried to formulate a definition of the family. Robert H. Lowie defined the family as a group based on material relations, rights and duties of parenthood, common habitation, and reciprocal relations between parents and children. On similar lines Ralph Linton defined the family as a group that involves marriage, rights and duties of parents and children. Both Lowie and Linton argued that the family is common to all types of human societies in the past as well as the present.

George Peter Murdock examined 192 societies and formulated a definition of the family. According to his definition: "The family is a social group characterised by common residence, economic co-operation, and reproduction. It includes both sexes, at least two of whom maintain a socially approved sexual relationship, and one or more children, own or adopted." Like Lowie and Linton, Murdock too concluded that the family can be found in all types of human societies in all places and in all times.

A careful examination of the early definitions of the family reveals that anthropologists felt that marriage, common residence, stipulation of domestic services and reproduction and reciprocal relations between parents and children are the necessary criteria for a group to be called the family.

Opinions were divided with regard to the occurrence of the family in all societies. Although some of the evolutionists of nineteenth century denied the occurrence of the family in the simplest and rudest societies, some other among them, besides non-evolutionists of the early twentieth century, argued for the occurrence of the family even in the simplest and rudest societies.

During the last three decades, anthropologists have tried to provide a definition of the family in terms of certain criteria which are considered as important by the societies themselves as by the anthropologists. Edmund Leach initiated the first effort in this context. He tried to give an admirable concise definition of the family but failed to provide one that would apply to all types of human societies. Instead, he enumerated the various characteristics of marriage as the family. According to him the criteria for a group to be called the family are: marriage, legal paternity and maternity, monopoly of the couple over each other's sexuality, rights of the spouses to each other's labour services, rights of both the spouses over property to establish a joint fund of property for the benefit of their children, and a socially significant relationship of affinity between each spouse and the relatives of the other. Leach concluded that since no single one of these criteria is invariably found in every known society, we ought to feel free to call the family any group which fulfils any one or more of these criteria.

Apart from Edmund Leach, anthropologists like Melford Spiro, Prince Peter of Greece and Denmark, Kathleen Gough and several others have tried their best to arrive at a definition of the family that is applicable to all societies but the problem of defining the family has, by no means, been resolved to the satisfaction of all. Levy and Fallers concluded that the family is a primary kinship unit which carries out aspects of the sexual, reproductive, economic and educational functions.

The above discussions reveals that although the anthropologists in the last three decades assumed that the family is somehow necessary and is, therefore, found in all human societies, there is little agreement with regard to what exactly constitutes the family and what precisely is the universally applicable definition of the family. William Newton Stephens tried to give a definition of the family that holds good to all human societies. According to his definition: "The family in general is a group based on marriage and marriage contact, including recognition of the rights and duties of parenthood, common residence for husband wife and children and reciprocal economic obligations between husband and wife."

Stephens definitions of the family rests on four criterias: marriage and marriage contract, reciprocal economic obligations between husband and wife, common residence and rights and duties of parenthood. Stephen says that not all these criterias can be found in every human society. The family in a vast majority of the societies satisfies all the criteria mentioned in the definition. However, there are a few societies in which the family may be formulated to make it applicable to all societies including even those societies which could not be covered by his definition of the family. This is what exactly Edmund Leach has said almost three decades ago. However, in the absence of such a definition of the family that has universal applicability, the definition of the family given by William Stephens may serve as an appropriate one for understanding the basic social group in a vast majority of the societies.

FUNCTION OF THE FAMILY

Sexual Function

The family includes the husband-wife relationship to fulfil a sexual function. Unlike most other female primates, the human female is, more or less, continuously receptive to sexual activity. The continuous female sexuality might have created a considerable sexual competition between males for females. Society might have prevented such competition in order to survive and it might have developed some way of minimizing the rivalry between males for females in order to reduce the chance of lethal conflict. Permanent paired mating, that is mating on a regular basis between people of opposite sex, might have become a solution to this problem. As a result marital unions, conjugal relationship or husband-wife relationship have come into existence. The husband-wife relationship has become a socially approved means to control sexual relation and a socially approved basis of the family. However, there are some exceptional cases where it is not the husband-wife relationship established by marriage, rather the father-mother relationship established by the foundation of the family, that grants sexual privileges to the males and females. For example, among the Banan of New Guinea and some of the peasant societies in Eastern Europe a groom is not permitted to approach his wife until she bears him a child by a special relative of his father. With the exception of such small number of society, in a vast majority of the societies, the family institutionalizes and channelizes the sexual outlets, and it gives each partner a monopoly in the sexuality of the other.

Economic Function

The family serves economic funtion also. Husband-wife relationship is not merely a sexual union, it is sexual union with economic co-operation. There are sexual unions without economic co-operation. There are also economic units without any sexual relationship between an employer and a secretary. The relationship between brother and sister is an example of economic union without sexual union. But husband-wife relationship exists only when the economic and sexual unions are considered into one relationship and this combination occurs only in the context of the family. The family entails both sexual and economic relationship. By virtue of sex difference the spouses make a unique and efficient co-operating unit. Man with his superior muscular strength undertakes more strenuous tasks. Woman with her physiological burdens of pregnancy and nursing performs lighter tasks. In all societies there is some kind of division of labour on the basis of sex. Each partner performs tasks according to sex-based division of labour. With the birth of off-spring the division of labour based on age and generation comes into play. As the children come up of age, they offer their parents considerable relief and help. Siblings are similarly bonded to one another, the care and help given by an elder to an younger, through co-operation in childhood games and through mutual economic assistances as they grow older. The cords of reciprocal economic obligations, tie together parents and children. In simpler societies where the family is a self-contained unit of production, consumption and distribution, it encompasses all economic roles characteristic of a society but in advanced societies where the family is not a self-contained unit of production, consumption and distribution, it includes only some of the economic roles charcteristic of a society. Thus, family serves economic functions.

Reproductive Function

The task of perpetuating the population of a society is an important function of the family. Sexual co-habitation between the spouses automatically leads to the birth of off-spring. The family nurses and rears its off-spring to physical and social maturity. However, there are some simpler societies which have a low rich rate of children and hence procure children from their neighbouring societies through frequent raids and rear them as their own children. In these societies the family does not perform the reproductive function as in other societies do. Not considering such exceptional cases, it may be said that a society reproduces itself biologically through the family.

Educational Function

The family fulfils a educational function. The young human, in fact, must acquire an immense amount of traditional knowledge and skill and must learn to subject his inborn impulses to the many disciplines prescribed by his society, before he can assume his place as an adult member of his society. The burden of enculturation and education falls primarily upon the family. The task of enculturating and educating the children is distributed between the parents. The father alone is capable of training the sons in the divisions of labour by sex. He alone is capable of training the sons in the activities and disciplines of adult males. Likewise the mother alone is capable of training the daughter in the activities and disciplines of adult females. Older siblings also play an important role imparting knowledge and discipline through daily interaction in work and play. There are a few societies in which the family does not undertake the enculturative and educative functions. For example, in some societies in West Africa and Austrialia there are bush schools, where youths receive instruction in tribal culture for several years and acquaint themselves with many cultural aspects of their society. In many advanced societies the educational function is performed by the educational institution in the form of schools, colleges and universities. Even then the family continues to be to some extent the first school. Ignoring such exceptions, it may be said that in a vast majority of the societies collective responsibility for enculturation and education weds the various relationships of the family together.

Typology of the Family

Typology of the families means systematic classification of the families into several types. A typology of the families can be constructed on the basis of the criterion or form of marriage. The forms of marriage may be monogamy, polygyny and polyandry. They are based on the number of male or female spouses involved in each union. Taking the different forms of marriages as the basis, the families can be classified into different types: Monogamous families, polygynous families and polyandrous families.

Another typology of families can be built on the basis of the criterion of descent. The term descent refers to the way in which one acquires membership of a kinship group. If the descent is traced through father in every generation it is called *patrilineal descent* or *agnatic descent*; if the descent is traced through mother in each generation, it is called *matrilineal descent* or *uterine descent*. If a person traces descent through both mother and father on each generation it is called *bilateral descent*. If one traces descent through mother in one generation but through father in another generation it is called *ambilineal descent*. According to the types of descent we may classify the families into several types: *patrilineal families, matrilineal families, bilateral families* and *ambilineal families*. If it is a patrilineal family,

MARRIAGE AND FAMILY IN PRIMITIVE SOCIETIES

one may trace his ancestry through his father; if it is a matrilineal family, one may trace ancestry through one's mother; if it is a bilateral family, one may trace your ancestry through both father and mother; and if it is an ambilineal family, one may trace one's ancestry through father in one generation but in the next generation one's son may trace ancestry through his mother, that is, his wife.

A different typology of the families can also be constructed with the help of the criterion of residence. The term residence refers to post-marital residence. If residence is with or near the groom's parents it becomes *patrilocal* or *virilocal* (Latin=vir=male, locus=place); if it is with or bride's parents it becomes *matrilocal* or *uxorilocal* (Latin:uxori=wife, locus=place); if it is either with or near groom's parents or with or near bride's parent it is called *bilocal* or *ambilocal* (Latin; ambi=both, locus=place); if it is with or near groom's mother's brother, it is called avuneulocal, and if the couple sets up a new household removed to some degree from the relatives of either the bride or the groom, it is called *neolocal* (Greek: neo=new, locus=place) residence. According to these patterns of residence the families can be classified into several types: *patrilocal* families, matrilocal families, bilocal families, avunculocal family and *neolocal* families.

A distinct typology of the families can be built by using authority as a critirion. The term authority refers to the right to have power or commanding influence over the members of the family. If the authority is in the father, it is called *paternal authority* and if it is vested in the mother, it is called *maternal authority*. According to these two types of authority the families can be classified into two types: *paternal families* and *maternal families*. In paternal families authority runs in the male line. It is vested generally in the eldest male living or in the eldest son. In maternal families authority runs in the female lines. It is vested in the eldest female living or in the eldest daughter.

Types of succession also can be used for constructing a typology of the families. The transmission of office or rank is called *succession*. Succession may be patrilineal or matrilineal. *Matrilineal succession* means the passing of titles or ranks from females to females. *Patrilineal succession* means the passing of titles or ranks from males to males. Accordingly the families may be classified into *patrilineal families* and *matrilineal families*.

The families can also be classified into several types on the basis of composition of relatives or relatives or kinship structure. That means the families can be classified by determining how many *father-offspring* or *mother-off-spring* units are linked with particular women or men respectively. A family that has one *father-offspring* unit linked with a woman or *mother-offspring* unit linked with a man is called *single family, elementary family, simple family, atomistic family, immediate family* or *nuclear family*. A family that has more than one father-off spring unit or mother-offspring unit linked with particular woman or men is called a *composite family*. The *composite family* may contain several sub-types. If the composite family has more than one mother-offspring unit linked with several men, it becomes *polyandrous family*; if it has more than one father-offspring unit linked with several women; it becomes *polygynous family;* if it has more than one father-offspring unit each linked with a woman or more than one *mother-offspring unit each linked, it is called an extended* family.

The following table gives the various types of families classified on the basis of specific criteria such as marriage, descent, residence, authority and composition or kinship structure.

Specific Criterion	*Types of the families*
Marriage	
Monogamy	Monogamous family.
Polygyny	Polygynous family.
Polyandry	Polyandrous family.
Descent	
Patrilineal	Patrilineal family.
Matrilineal	Matrilineal family.
Ambilineal	Ambilineal family.
Bilateral	Bilateral family.

Residence
Patrilocal   Patrilocal family.
Matrilocal   Matrilocal family.
Bilocal   Bilocal family.
Avunculocal   Avunculocal family.
Neolocal   Neolocal family.

Authority
Paternal   Paternal family.
Maternal   Maternal family.

Succession
Patrilineal   Patrilineal family.
Matrilineal   Matrilineal family.

Composition
One father,
Offspring or mother and   Nuclear family.
Offspring unit linked with
a mother or a father
More than one father
one mother-offspring or
mother-offspring unit   Composite family.
linked with women and men.

Typology Based on Multiple Criteria

The typologies of families, each based on a single criterion, are not complete ones for two reasons. First, each single criterion employed to classify the families into distinct types takes into consideration only one aspect of the family, either marriage or descent of residence or authority or structure at a time, without simultaneously taking into consideration the various aspects of the family. Second, each single criterion cannot be considered as having universal applicability. That is, each criterion cannot be successfully employed to classify the families existing in all types of human societies in all places, at all times. Therefore, multiple criteria are to be employed for evaluating a satisfactory typology of the families.

George Peter Murdock, Radcliffe-Brown and several other anthropologists have constructed separate typologies of families on the basis of multiple criteria, such as forms of marriage, patterns of residence and networks of kin relations (Murdock and Radcliffe-Brown). The typology of families envolved by Murdock is most commonly used by anthropologists in studying household arrangements in different societies across the globe. The following chart shows the types of families constructed by George Peter Murdock:

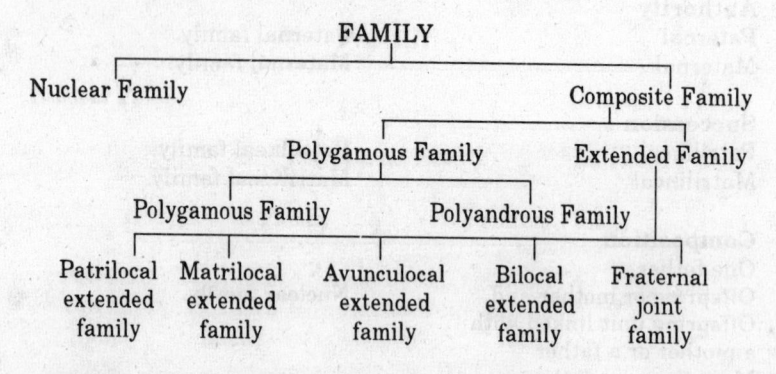

```
                           FAMILY
        ┌────────────────────┴──────────────────────┐
   Nuclear Family                              Composite Family
                              ┌────────────────────┴─────────┐
                        Polygamous Family              Extended Family
                   ┌──────────┴──────────┐                   │
           Polygamous Family      Polyandrous Family         │
        ┌──────┬──────────┬──────────┬──────────┐
    Patrilocal  Matrilocal  Avunculocal  Bilocal   Fraternal
    extended    extended    extended     extended   joint
    family      family      family       family     family
```

The nuclear family consists of a married man and woman with their offspring although in individual cases one or more additional persons may reside with them.

One *composite family* is an aggregation of two or more nuclear families. It may be divided into two types: The *polygamous family* and the *extended family*. The *polygamous family* consists of two or more nuclear families affiliated by plural marriages, i.e., by having one married parent in common. In this context the plural marriage may be polygyny or polyandry.

An *extended family* consists of two or more nuclear families affiliated through an extention of the parent-child relationship. Depending upon post-marital residence, an extended family may be *patrilocal, matrilocal, bilocal* and *avunculocal*. The patrilocal extended family consists of two or more nuclear families affiliated through an extention of father-son relationship. The *Matrilocal extended family* consists of two or more nuclear families affiliated through an extension of mother-daughter relationship. The *bilocal extended family*, which is also known as *ambilocal extended family*, is a combination of *patrilocal extended family* and *matrilocal extended family*. The *avunculocal extended family* consists of two or more nuclear families affiliated through an extension of maternal-uncle and sister's son relationship. It includes the nuclear family formed by a man and his wife and daughters, and the nuclear families formed by his sister's son and their wives and children.

The patrilocal extended families are most common form which involves each three generations of kin living together, viz. parents, their children and the families of their children. If the parents die, their children may remain together often with several brothers heading the family. This form of extended family, which involves the joining of two or more sibling's families is known as the *fraternal joint families*. The fraternal joint families are also found in China and Pakistan. In Pakistan it is called *Khumbah*; in Yugoslavia, Romania and Bulgaria, it is known as *Zadruga*. The joint family among the *Tanala* of Medagascar is similar to a patrilocal extended family.

Apart from these most common types of extended family, there are some uncommon types of extended family, such as *matrifocal* families, consanguineal families and *stem* families confined to a few society in different parts of the world. A *matrifocal family* is an extended family which includes a woman, her daughter and her daughers' children and sometimes several female relatives such an aunts, nieces, cousin sisters or grandmothers. A matrifocal family is characterized by the absence of permanent adult male members. This type of family is found in Jamaica, Naity, Guyana and other Carabean countries.

The consanguineal is an extended family which includes a woman, her son, her daughters, her daughters' children. However, it does not include son's wife and their children. Thus, a consanguineal family consists of a woman, her brothers and her offspring.

The stem family is a kind of patrilineal extended family, which includes an old couple, one of their son, one of their son's wife and one of their son's children. It is, however, found among some of the farming population of Europe.

Persistence and changes in the Family

Though the family, as an institution is permanent and

universal in all human societies, it has undergone certain changes within itself as an association. Thus, compositional and structural changes sometimes take place within a family organization. The modern type of family found among both castes and tribes of India, is a typical example of this kind of change. The traditional joint family has changed over to the small joint family or nuclear family in the recent decades of this century, but this change has been basically structural. The functions of the family, however, have not been much disturbed in spite of the structural changes in the family. Under the impact of urbanization and industrialization and other processes of change, the concept of family has undergone drastic transformations not only in India but all over the world. But in spite of the changes in the form and structure of the family, family as an institution continues in one way or the other, all over the world and it will continue so long as human beings exist.

CHAPTER IV

Kinship System

Kinship is defined as the connection or relationship between persons by blood or marriage. If the kin is related by blood, it is called consanguineal kinship relation. For example, father-son relationship will be called consanguineal kinship relation. Similarly, when the kins are related by marriage or by affinal relationship, the kinship relation is called affinal. The husband and wife relationship is called affinal relationship.

All societies recognise these kinship relationship with certain limitation. In primitive societies, kinship relations are broad based and hence it is called broad range kinship. Again cognates are persons descended from the same ancestors or ancestress. Then the cognates may be traced either in the male line or female line. If cognates are traced in male line, they are referred to as agnates and their relationship as patrilineal kinship or agnatic kinship. If cognates are traced in female line, they are referred to as uterine kin and their relationship is known as matrilineal kinship.

Type of Kin Group

Kinship terminology forms an important part in the whole kinship system as it serves as an index to understanding of the kinship relation and patterns of behaviour among various kin groups. Its origin is as old as the origin of anthropology itself as a science of man. To an extent, it was acknowledged about different kinship system of the world that initially introduced interest in the study of man and culture.

Kinship groups are usually classified into two broad groups, viz—classificatory kins and the affinal kins, about which we have referred to earlier. Now we discuss them one by one.

The Classificatory Kin Groups

Before we discuss the classificatory and descriptive kingroup, we would like to explain some of the diagrammatic representation of kinship for scientific understanding of the kinship system with special reference to the kinship ties.

△ - Male   O - Female
= - Affinal or Marital tie
- - Consanguineal tie
I - Line of descent

Let us draw typical nuclear family using the above symbol.

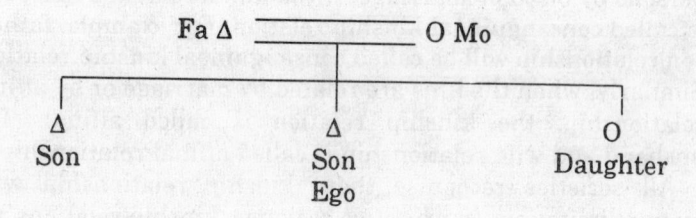

```
       Fa △ ─────────── O Mo
             │
      ┌──────┼──────┐
      △      △      O
     Son    Son   Daughter
            Ego
```

It was Morgan who first discovered a system of kinship address, which classified a number of people together under a common term of address. During his studies of the Iroquois, Morgan had come to know that among a primitive people like them a kinship term may be used to designate a number of persons. Morgan discussed in his treatise that among many people, it is assumed that all who live together or make up the home circle are related to each other in some way, and it is considered that other groups are related among themselves in the same way. If men stay at home and their wives come from outside, all men of one's generation will be called by the same term which means brother; and all woman by the same term which means sister. Thus, Morgan came to discover that one's own father, his brothers and cousins, and even more remotely related men of his generations are called by the same common term, which means 'father'. The same thing happens with the other side of the family; the mother, her sister cousins on her side, and so on, will all be 'mothers'.

This type of kinship system, Morgan termed as the classificatory system of kinship, since it refers to a number or class of persons. It is also called the Dakota type of nomenclature after the name of the people (Dakota) among whom it was first discovered.

In a classificatory or Dakota type of kinship system, one single term is used for a set of persons, standing in different types of relation to the ego and among themselves. They may even be too remote to be so recognised. The simplest and, perhaps, a highly developed form of kinship system is found in a Maori village where all the grandparents' generation are grandparents', all of the father's generations are 'fathers', all of the mother's generations are 'mothers', all of one's own generation are 'brothers' and 'sisters', and persons of one's children's generation are called 'my children'. To quote another example from the Tamilion society, mother's brother, father of sister's husband and father-in-law, all are addressed by the same kinship term *Mama*, because of cross-cousin marriage prevalent in the society. The Sema Nagas have a specific term *Angu* to address a number of persons, viz., mother's brother, mother's brother's children (both son and daughter), husband's father and wife's father, husband's brother and wife's brother.

Sinha (1964) has shown that among the Buguns of NEFA, the kinship term *Mukhan* is used for two different sets of relationship; for father's elder brother and mother's elder sister. The term surpasses the distinction of sex in the first place, and secondly, the remarkable differences between two different degrees of relation—the paternal and maternal kin; it also marks the attitudinal behaviour. It is further suggested that mother's elder sister may be held in the same esteem of respect and proximity of relationship as one's father's elder brother. This has a special significance in the context of a patrilineal society like the Bugun where paternal kins are regarded nearer in relation that the maternal ones. This also suggests in a way a bilateral system of reckoning descent.

The system seems to further imply that marriage with mother's elder sister's daughter or son is avoided in the same way as with elder brother's son or daughter. This is indeed proved by other kinship terms as well. The term of kinship address is the same as for one's own sister, Memua, thus suggesting that the form falls equally in the forbidden degree of marital relations as the latter.

Again, one's mother's sister's son is called by the same term, *Kolafua*, as one's father's brother's son, brother's son, and one's own son; this seems to be an interesting grouping of three generations. This dispels the possibility for parallel cousin marriage of one type with mother's sister's son or daughter. The parallel cousin marriage of the other type, with one's father's brother's son or daughter, is disapproved by the fact that father's brother's son falls in the same group of kinship address as brother's son or one's own son besides mother's sister's son.

The Sema Nagas have a classificatory term of address—*Aja*—for mother, father's brother's wife and mother's sister. The first two are indicative of levirate and the first and the third of sororate. The term *Apu* used for father, father's brother and mother's sister's husband, indicates marriage of several sisters to husbands who are brothers. Again, *Ami* is used for father's sister, wife's mother husband's mother and husband's brother's wife. The first two terms basically indicate cross-cousin marriage. It is significant that the term of address for father and mother which are usually descriptive in most societies became classificatory among the Sema Nagas. Classificatory system of kinship also prevails among the Kuki clans, the Angami Nagas, etc.

The Descriptive Kin Groups

L.H. Morgan refers to another form of kinship system as prevalent commonly in the Western societies and in which a single kinship term refers only to a particular individual and specific kind of relationship. This is known as *descriptive* kin terms, which is different from the classificatory kin term. We very commonly speak of uncles and aunts or cousins in a classificatory way but without designating the exact relationship. For example, the term father explains the exact blood relationships, but the word uncle or the word *Mama* does not explain any blood relationship. If the former is to be called *descriptive* kin term, the latter will be called *classificatory* kin term.

L.H. Morgan had assigned the following characteristics of the descriptive kin terms:
   (a) that the terms express blood relationship and are applicable to person having actual blood relationship with the speaker.
   (b) that the collateral lines are kept distinct from each other and divergent from the linear; the terms nephew and niece are applied to persons related collaterally, the divergence of successive generations being indicated in the names employed.
   (c) that in most cases, except for the nearer relatives, the terms are essentially descriptive.

In the descriptive kinship system the terms usually referred to the single biological family comprising of man, wife and children. The term of address for other social relation, not directly involved in this family which are usually vague and indefinite, are not included in the descriptive kinship system.

The classificatory system, on the other hand, reckons kinship between groups rather than individuals, the collateral lines are not kept distinct and divergent from the lineal.

Morgan had also suggested that the kinship terminology cannot be "borrowed", and any similarity would adduce it to the migration of people from one place to another.

Kinship Behaviour

Some of the usages, which have social sanction and convention are considered necessary for keeping order and decorum in society. Those usages which are related to behaviours between kin relations are called as kinship behaviours. In the society, there are different types of families and various degrees of kin groups exhibit different types of behaviour by cutting joke with each other or perform avoidance relationship, and such usages, verbal or known verbal, constitute kinship behaviour, some of these kinship behaviours which are universally found are avoidance and joking relationship, avunculate, amitate, couvade and teknonymy.

Avoidance

Many societies all over the world observed a kind of restrained or avoidance behaviour towards a daughter-in-law, towards a mother-in-law, father-in-law, younger brother's wife, etc. Similarly, some kind of avoidance is shown in between son-in-law and his mother-in-law, etc.

Some theorists and scholars have given various explanations for these types of avoidance. Tylor was probably the first to explain it and he was of opinion that in the early stages of human history, when sons-in-law used to live with their wives in a matriarchal society, they were obliged to have restricted relation with their mothers'-in-law. Tylor suggested that in the beginning society was in matriarchal form and hence-this avoidance behaviour was essential.

Frazer has given his explanation of the avoidance based on evidences drawn from one of the very primitive Ceylonese tribe, the Vedda, where brother-sister avoidance prevails, and from the Trobriand Islanders among whom very limited social relation exists between brothers and sisters. Frazer suggests that the purposes of this avoidance is to prevent such sexual intimacy as would amount to incest.

Freud also took great interest interpreting avoidance through his usual psycho-analytical approach. He also, like Frazer, regards sexual attraction and the subsequent need to prevent sexual intimacy between some kin relations at the root of such avoidance.

Lowie has given more reasonable explanation of avoidance. He says a daugher-in-law represents an alien and perhaps a different set off social, cultural, and moral value. She is different in her language, dresses, beliefs, notions and manners and etiquette from her husband's family. Her husband is found to be influenced by her, but the rest of his family is not and hence avoidance relationship is practiced. Radcliffe Brown has given perhaps, the most plausible explanation of this avoidance behaviour. To him avoidance is a social fact and must, therefore, have a social explanation. He believes that whenever people come into contact and interact with other people, the possibilities of co-operation as well as conflict equally arise. But at the same time there may always be certain kinds of kinship where hostility is regarded as against social norms. The best way to prevent such hostility from becoming manifest is to put restrictions in the growth of intimacy and to ensure this kinship behaviour of avoidance is necessary.

Joking Relationship

Societies have sometimes diametricaly opposite attitudes or behaviour patterns. One such opposite to the attitude of avoidance is relationship of an extreme degree of familiarity expressed through joking relationship between certain kin relations. Such joking may amount to deep satire, taunt, exchange of abuse, obscene and vulgar references to sex. Sometimes they express themselves in social ridicule and do deliberate damage to each other personality. Various socio-anthropological explanations have been given to explain this queer usage of familiarity.

Joking relationship may indicate equality and mutual reciprocity between the two kins indulging in it. They may also be sometimes indicatives of potential sexual relationship. This is particularly true of the joking relationship between a man and his wife's younger sister or between a woman and her husband's younger brother. Both types of relations are potential mates. A joking relationship with one's mother's brother's wife may indicate the practice of inheriting all the property of one's mother's brother, which is sarcastically enough to include his wife too. Joking relationship of these kinds are reported from matrilineal Hopi and the matrilineal Trobriand Islanders. Some societies have joking relationships between grand parents and grandchildren. The Oraons and the Baigas are two such examples reported by S.C. Roy and Verrier Elwin. S.C. Roy reported an instance of a grandfather marrying his grand daughter among Oraon of Bihar. Verrier Elwin has reported a similar case from the Baigas of Madhya Pradesh, where a grandson married his own grandmother.

A joking relationship, when not reciprocal, exercises a social control as it exercises correction through ridicule. Radcliffe Brown made a special study of joking relationship among some of the African tribes. He regards the joking relationship as having a symbolic meaning. Joking relations may be only a kind of friendliness expressed by a show of hostility. Chapple and Coon regard this kinship behaviour as a medium to stimulate a higher interaction rate between various people which may not be possible to do if otherwise.

Couvade

Couvade is, perhaps, the most queer usage of the primitive society, though it has much social significance in many preliterate and primitive societies of the world. In couvade, the husband of the wife, who has given birth to a child, presumes himself to be sharing his wife's agony and lives a parallel confinement with her. Such a practice has been reported from among the Khasi and Toda tribes of India. Instances elsewhere in several parts of the world are also found. This sharing of a kinship usage by the husband and wife both, has been explained variously by the scholars. Some of the authorities have seen in this usage the survival of the transitional stage of the maternal-paternal complex.

Malinowski believes that couvade is a cementing bond of married life and a social mechanism devised to secure paternal affection. Raglan regards it as an irrational belief, which may be prior to marriage, and be even a contributory cause of the emergence of marriage as an institution.

Some of the other writers have sought to give a psycho-analytical explanation; they attribute this usage to the husband's desire to lighten his wife's discomforts by a process of participation through identification. Lately some other explanations have also been argued for. It is suggestd that a woman, who has delivered a child, undergoes certain chemical processes within her body which affect the atmosphere around her, particularly if she is in an ill-ventilated cell, she thus makes all inhabitants living in it highly prone to sickness emanting from her. Viewed in this light, couvade does not appear a primitive or superstitious usage. This seems a more rational explanation of the usage though it is not yet fully corraborated by ethnographic evidences.

The kinship usages are significant in as much as they reveal some kinship or institutional behaviour; they are only a part of some larger social complex, and are never independent.

Avunculate

In all those societies, where wife stays at her home and husband goes to live with her or visits her occassionally, wife's brother acts as the head of the household and exercises authoritative rights over his sister's children and this convention becomes known as avunculate and the maternal uncle's authority is called *avuncupotestability*. The maternal uncle has a primary social obligation to exercise towards his nephew and nieces and not towards his own children, and in turn, they also respect him most, even more than their own father, obey his authority and work for him. They also become heir to their maternal uncle's property. This kinship usage prevails basically in matrilineal societies.

Amitate

Similarly, there is another kinship usage known as *amitate* prevalent in patrilineal societies where father's sister becomes prominent in matters of rights and authorities. Like mother's brother in a matriarchal society, the father's sister here acts virtually as the head of the household and exercises her supreme authority over her brother's children. This form of kinship behaviour was studied by Radcliffe Brown and I. Schapera [1] and they termed it *"Female-father"*. Whereas amitate is easily understandable in patrilineal organisation, but its occurrence among the matrilineal Trobriands, as reported by Malinowski, is a curious instance.

Teknonymy

In many rural societies of India, it is quite common whether as a part of some orthodoxy or some convention to call or to refer to, one's child as the father or mother of his or her child. This usage is called *Teknonymy*. It is also shared by the Tribal people like the Khasis of Meghalaya and by other primitive societies of the world. Tylor has taken keen interest to explain this phenomenon. He suggests that it is a relic of some old stage in culture history, when some women were supreme in position and authority and who never accepted the son-in-law as one of them in their houses. According to Tylor, they recognise only a secondary relationship through the children he raised for the home. As an extention of this, a mother may also be referred to teknonymously. Thus it is a type of relationship which is designated through extention.

Moiety, Phratry and Clan

Phratry and moiety are two common terms used in kinship organisation. Phratry is derived from Greek word "Phrater", which means brother. Thus a phratry is a kin group of brotherhood in which there are several clans combined together. In some societies two or more clans are united or even in larger groups all members sharing a tradition of common descent. A phratry is thus a consanguineous group. Sub-divided moiety are also known as phratry, but a phratry need not be a moiety. Finally, it may be concluded that while moiety is a bigger unit of the tribe, the phratry is a small one. Further, it may be said that in a moiety there may be a number of phratries. In our Hindi vernacular, moiety is called *"ardhansha"* (half) while phratry is understood as *bhratra-samuh.*

A tribe may have moieties and phratries both. A phratry is also explained as it consists of several clans. Thus in a phratry, there may be a number of clans. In this way when we compare phratry and clans, we see that phratry is a bigger unit than the clan. In another word different clans may occur in a phratry. Lowie suggests several possibilities for such combination. He says several clans may combine together without loosing all survivals of their previous separateness, or a clan may grow so large that it splits up into lesser groups without completely severing the former bonds of unity. Instances of both these types of fusion and fission, are found among some of the tribes of Chotanagpur region of Bihar, specially among the Oraon, the Ho and other cognate tribes of the Mund region.

Another possibility suggests that a clan organisation may be totally extinct in course of time. W.H.R. Rivers had reported such a situation from among the Todas of Nilgiri Hills of South India, which have a dual organisation and which has come into existence as their clan groups which were large in numbers and got gradually extinct in course of time.

Lowie has further pointed out that clans and moiety may arise there separately for separate region, but may, later combine into one organisation, though continuing to be part of the same social system. He cites some examples from some of the American-Indian tribes.

The word "moiety", has been derived from the French word *Moietic* which means half. Such a society where moiety is found is said to be having dual organisation. Each moiety may be named after some totemic object, animate or inanimate. Murdock (1949) has reported about the matrilineal exogamous moieties of some of the American-Indian tribes of the North-West Pacific coasts. Some other American-Indians are known to have moieties named after natural dualities, like sky and earth, winter and summer, etc. Moieties are generally based on descent and are exogamous rules which serve as a useful means for organising the societies and for guiding the individual in his inter-personal relationships.

As mentioned above, there are many clans found in a phratry. Clan has a widely and variously organised system. The clan organisation differs from one part of the world to the other. Taking this diversity of clans or sib in view, we may broadly classify them into three main types:

(i) Territorial Organised Clans,
(ii) Totemic Clans, and
(iii) Clans knowingly nicknames.

The clans may be organised territorially and they may be spread over a particular territory and members of such a clan may be confined to a particular area. The Ollar-Gudbas (Jha, 1972, 1983) of Koraput, Orissa, are a typical example of the territorial clans. Similarly the Nagas of Meghalaya are also territorially organised in the areas, having sub-divisions known as *Khels*.

The second type of clan organisation is one organised on a totemic basis. The Murias of Bustar are divided into four clans on a totemic basis much as Marami, Naitam, Poyam and Sodi, which have their associated totem in goats and tigers, etc.

The clans named after some nicknames are found mostly among the Australian tribes. The crow-Indians of America are also divided into 13 exogamous mother sibs. These units are designated after nicknames. The crows were locally divided into northern and southern branch, but in each were found members of all the sibs.

The sibs or clans may be thus organised on any of these bases or divided into half in the form of a dual organisation and give right to moieties.

The clan is, as we have discussed above, a group of selected kins by birth, The members of the clan cannot change the clan by choice. It has many functions in the society about which different anthropologists have given their different arguments.

Many of their expected functions are defined in clear terms, but several functions are followed conventionally or largely out of realization of their serving some wider functions. One basic function not so well defined, is to unite the different inmates of the group into a solidarity group by creating in them a feeling of oneness. The different functions of the clan can be best explained by the ethnographic examples. The Hopi sibs of Northern Arizona are matronymic and extrogamous, father and son are never in the same sib, hence a father cannot pass on his ceremonial privileges to his own child but transmits them to his nearer relatives viz. his brother's or his sister's son. In this way property is transferred due to clan-organisation. The clan may also be a local or non-local unit, a political or non-political division of the societies in some cases. As the clans are always exogamous, it has a great role to play in the settlement of marriage. Thus a clan performs many important functions in the tribal society not only at the level of negotiating marriages but also at the level of organising ceremonies, rituals, fairs and festivals which are performed at the clan level.

Clans are also associated with totemism. The members of the clan believe that the clan men have descended from a common ancestor who is symbolically represented by an object of veneration or worship who may be animal or a plant. These clans bear the names of associated animals or plants or other natural phenomena. For example, among the Ollar-Gudba of Koraput, Orissa, there were clans named after *Bagh* (Tiger), *Mina* (Fish), etc., and the members of which were known as *Min-Bansh, Bagh-Bansh,* etc.

Totemism makes the clan-organisation more complex, but at the sametime, it also perhaps, makes it more interesting. In the tribal societies of India, clan is universally found among them, but there are some exceptions. The Maler of Rajmahal hills of Santhal Pargana, Bihar, is such a tribe where clan is not found (Vidyarthi, 1963). The functions of clan among the Maler are performed by the lineages.

The lineage is unilineal descent group composed of all those consanguineous kins to whom the individual can trace "an actual geneological tie". In those circumstances where descent is reckoned patrilineally, the resulting consanguineous descent group is called a patrilineage. If the descent is matrilineal, the similarly resulting consangiuineous descent group is called matrilineous. Patrilineous and matrilineous are essentially exogamous kin-groups.

Rules of Descent

Kinship can be based on *bilateral descent* as well as *unilateral descent.* Generally, there are three rules of descent from both the parents and the later through either of the parent—thus *patrilineal* and *matrilineal;* hence these rules of bilateral descent assign a person to a close group of kinsmen to whom he is related through both sides, males and females. *Patrilineal descent* affiliates him with a group in which descent is traced only through males. *Matrilineal descent* connects him with a group related only through females in those societies, which follow double descent, a person may be assigned simultaneously to two groups, one patrilineal and the other matrilineal.

It is not yet determined that which of these basic three systems developed first in the cultural history of man. It has only been possible to identify some of the cultural circumstances with which each system may have been recurrently associated, thereby suggesting a casual co-relation that appears to be significant.

While discussing the family, we have seen that the rule of *post-nuptial* residence that determines the domestic group is primarily determined by the patterns of a people's techno-economic adaptation. The hunters and some of the developed farmers may have found that in the male work solidarity is more important for them. This is, clearly seen in their control of allocation of goods and their role in offence and defence, that are most critical to the maintenance and protection of their ways of life. This seems to be directly reflected in the high incidence of the virilocal residence rule which, ultimately produces the patrilocal family among all such peoples.

Among the horticulturists, where women have to do most of the gardening and other associated domestic work, matrilocal families are found. The threat of warfare and intertribal of inter-communal feuds is less in such societies. Therefore, the need for male solidarity is comparatively less emphasized. The rarer rule of uxorilocal post-nuptial residence occurs most commonly in such societies.

The residence rule has a tendency to be bilocal where the techno-environmental adaptation is unstable enough or where the techno-economic positions of men and women are so nearly equivalent that a more flexible rule of *post-nuptial* residence is found to be most adaptative.

These observations indirectly prove the thesis that rules of descent appear to be solely determined by rules of residence. Residence rules and descent rules both reflect the pattern of a people's techno-environmental and techno-economic adaptation. They are formed by these conditions and are reinforced by cultural conditions and tradition; incourse, they are particularly governed by the political system and by the ideology behind it. They may act back upon these other aspects of culture, sometimes inhibiting and sometimes directing their development. In some cases the rules of residence and descent themselves give way to the pressures for technological innovation and economic change, and they begin to change.

The Bilateral Descent

Bilateral kinship is significant particularly because of the fact that it recognizes both kinds of kindred, paternal as well as maternal. Moreover, it may extend to more than four generations. This is more so if the descent is symmetrical and the individual is related to four grandparents. The principle can even be potentially, extended further laterally and multiplied geometrically in each ascending generation, thus relating him to all third and fourth cousins and all eight great-grandparents.

In practice, this potentially enormous aggregation is very often "too inclusive" to be socially useful and pared down, and usually too small a group of close kinsmen to whom the person can accurately trace a genealogical tie.

The modern family, both of the West and the East, generally recognizes kinship through both the parents. It remains, however, a fact that this recognition may not be taken into cognisance or perpetuated in the names of the offspring.

In primitive and preliterate societies, however, other kinds of descent are also recognized. Thus, there may be sibs in a society which completely ignore one of the two lines of descent and are, consequently, called *unilateral* group.

Double Descent

As distinct, and almost opposite, to such groups are double descent and bilineal kin groups. The latter groups consists of only those persons who are related to ego through both patrilineal and matrilineal ties. In a double descent group, it is necessary that some kin representing each line is included. And individual may belong to a pair of such groups. He is affiliated through the agnatic line with his consanguineous kinsman who shared descent from a common male ancestor. At the same time, he may also be related through the uterine line, with a group of kinsmen who trace their descent from a common ancestress. As a result of this twofold recognition, the individual belongs to two, rather than one, consanguineous kin groups, one patrilineal and the other matrilineal.

In tracing the nature of relationship some rules are followed in the society. For example, if the relationship is traced through a common ancestor, the person bound together through this relationship is a man, they are called agnates or agnatic kin, sometimes also as patrilineal kin. The descendents of a woman ancestress are called uterin kin or matrilineal kin. The kin, who are related to each other directly through some descent are called lineal kin and those who branch out from the main group like uncle and cousins, are called collateral kin. Bilateral descent is not so much widespread. The unilateral descent is, however, more prevalent.

Unilateral Descent

The unilateral descent reckons descent through only one parent, the father or the mother. Thus special social significance is attributed to the biological tie through one parent. The individual in such society is assigned membership of a particular consanguineous kin group right from his birth. If the descent is traced unilineally through the father, the individual is affiliated with a consanguineous kin group through the male or agnatic line and the rule of descent becomes patrilineal. If the descent is traced unilineally through the mother, the individual is considered related with a consanguineous kin through the female or uterine line, the rule of descent becomes matrilineal.

Degree of Kinship

If a person is related to ego directly, then he is ego's primary kin. For example, one's father is one's primary consanguineous kin and one's wife is one's primary affinal kin.

Any kin related to ego through primary kin themselves being primary kin of ego's primary kin, are kin of the secondary degree. For example, father's brother or ego's step mother are ego's secondary consanguineous kin and secondary affinal kin respectively. Similarly one's wife's brother is one's affinal secondary kin.

The secondary kin of our primary kin or the primary kin of our secondary kin will be our tertiary kin. According to Murdock (1949), there are eight primary kins of an individual, thirtythree secondary kins and 151 tertiary kins.

Thus, in the kinship system, the degree of kinship is of three types as discussed above, through which the relationships are traced to establish the social solidarity among the members of the ethnic groups.

A kinship system may be called a broad range kinship or a narrow range according to a number of persons it includes.

The modern Western kinship system is a narrow range system, whereas the primitive kinship system is a broad range system including people scattered over relatively large areas between whom it is not possible to trace relationship without bringing in a mythical common ancestor. Thus, so far as kinship range is concerned, it is of two types as referred to above.

Reference

1. For detail see R. Brown and I. Schapera's jointly written book—*African System of Kinship and Marriages.*

CHAPTER V

Economic Anthropology

Meaning and Scope

Economic anthropology envisages economic activities of primitive man in his social and cultural framework. In other words, we can say that economic anthropology is an analysis of economic life as a sub-system of societies. Firth (1951) is of opinion that economic anthropology deals of social relations. Economy is an important constituent of the community life and play a deciding role in the formation of the cultural and social structure of the societies. As a matter of fact, the economic life of the tribal people helps us to understand an important feature of their culture.

Economic anthropology is the major sub-field of social anthropology, which deals with the way groups of people play in the tribal societies and obtained a living, from nature and with the factors affecting the organisation of those engaged in such activities. It also deals with the distribution of goods and services in societies and attempts to explain who gets what and why?

Economic anthropology is different from general economics because it deals primarily with primitive and peasant societies in which the economy is organised significantly with different than what it is in an industrialized society. Thus, economic anthrpologists have to re-examine the fundamental notions which economists take for granted. However, among the primitive economy the important subjects of study are the concepts of labour, production and consumption, barter and ceremonial exchange, value in non-monetary economic system, etc., which are the sources of major theoretical arguments over which scholars life Herskovits, Ramond Firth, Salisbury, Polanyi, Malinowski, etc., have done significant works.

Another difference between economic anthropology and classical economics is that while the latter is normally concerned with problems of distribution, because these dominate in industrialized economics, anthropologists studying primitive and peasant societies are forced to pay more attention to small-scale production.

Because of a simpler division of labour, this is much more important that distribution. Production for consumption is typically organised on a domestic level. It is inextricably linked to familial concerns and is at the same time extremely complex. As a result, this type of production has registered theoretical analysis until the recent attempt by Sahlins.

Economic anthropology not only deals with the inner dynamics of primitive and peasant societies but also explores the involvement of these societies in national or world economics. Often it attempts to explain the success of failure of primitive societies in the wider economy. Studies of this type by anthropologists are often linked with evaluating or even guiding community development projects. Recently, however, the emphasis has turned from stressing the modernising effect of contact with wider-economics to concern with impoverishment which seems to follow the involvement of marginal societies with the wider economy.

Finally, it may be concluded that the meaning and scope of primitive economy may be traced deeply in the material wants of the people. The activities associated with fulfilment of material wants, as Herkovits suggests, constitutes as important part of the economic life of the tribal societies. In a tribal society, where the price system is normally absent and social tradition regulates the economic activities, the general economics theories meant for the complex societies, would hardly be applicable in the primitive societies.

For an assessment of tribal economy, special analytical concepts and meanings are necessary because social organisation and culture, kinship, political organization, religion, etc., affect economic organisation and performance so directly and sensitively in tribal societies that only a socio-economic approach, which considers explicitly the relationship between economy and society is capable of yielding inside view and generalization of any importance. This purpose is served fully by economic anthropology. This kind of study for the first time was done by Good Fellow among the Bantus. Thereafter, Raymond Firth studied (1939) the Tikopean economics. The social and religious setting of the economy is also accorded full recognition as an effective force in shaping the economic life of the tribal people, yet the focus of the discussion remains continuously on the economic implication of the data and on the economic institutions prevalent in the primitive societies.

Definitions of Primitive Economy

On the basis of these meanings and scope of primitive economy specially in the field of social anthropology, scholars have defined precisely the primitive economy, and some of these definitions are given below for the benefit of the students:

Ralph Piddington (1952) says "Economic system is designed to satisfy material wants of the people, to organise production, to control distribution and to determine the rights and claims of ownership within the community."

Raymond Firth (1952) is of the opinion that "Economic organization is a type of social action. It involves the combination of various kinds of human services with one another and with goods in such a way that they serve the given ends."

Majumdar and Madan (1956) believe that "It consists of the ordering an organisation of human relation and human efforts in order to procure as many of the necessities of day to day life as possible, with the expenditure of minimum efforts. It is attempted to secure the maximum satisfaction possible through adapting limited means to unlimited ends in an organized manner."

George Dalton (1971) argues that "All societies have structured arrangements to provide the material means of individual and community life. It is these structured rules that we call an economic system."

In brief, it can be said that the concept and meaning of economic system with special reference to the tribals may be defined that economic system may have two important things, viz., the mode and structure of production and its relations, and the process of distribution existing and operating in a given socio-political set up. The mode of production implies technique and organisation of economic activities relating to production. The structure of production means social-relations in the performance of production activities and in the process of distribution between different social groups of the tribal societies. Finally, it may be concluded that the mode of production in tribal economy is traditional, indigenous and culturally predominant. The tribal people are culturally a social unit and at the same time enterpriser, workers as well as producer and consumer, the system of distribution is linked to the barter system or to the mutual exchange or the least monetary system. The tribal people work hard to get their livelihood to meet the basic needs of life, like food, shelter, etc., as well as the social needs like the materials for *rites-de-passage*, through their economic performances. Herskovits has rightly said that an individual operating as a member of his society in terms of the culture of his group is the economic unit.

Characteristics of the Primitive Economy

There are many characteristics of the primitive economic system which have been enumerated by some of the scholars which are given below for the benefit of the students.

According to Dalton (1971), there are three important characteristics of the primitive economy, such as:

(a) *Small Economy*: It is this smallness of scale which is the fundamental characteristic of primitive life (Wilson, 1941; 10), that most (but not all) resources, goods and service transactions take place within a community of persons numbered in hundreds or thousands. There are two other factors which make tribal economics small in scale, (i) Frequently one or two staple items comprise usually large proportion of total produce. It is common for these important staples to be produced within the small framework of a tribe (ii) A relatively small number of goods and services is produced and acquired.

(b) *Simple technology compared to the industrialized economics:* The tools are either made by the user himself or are acquired free from a craftsman or from a manufacturing group.

(c) *Geographical or Cultural Isolation (comparatively):* Majumdar and Madan (1956) have found nine important traits of a primitive economy as noticed in the tribal India and elsewhere.

There is an absence of technological aids in a tribal economy which results in inefficient, inadequate or even wasteful exploitation of nature. Consequently, the bare minimum necessary for sustenance is raised with great difficulty. An economic surplus is rare in their community.

The economic relations among the tribals themselves are mostly based on bartar and exchange, money as a store and measurement of value and medium of exchange is not used widely. Institutions like banking and credit are used only in dealing with non-tribal groups which depends upon the nature and frequency of contacts with them.

The profit motive in economic dealings is generally absent. The role of an incentive is fulfilled by a sense of mutual obligation, sharing and solidarity.

Co-operative and collective endeavour is a strongly developed feature of their economy.

The rate of innovation, internal or induced, is very low and consequently they are stabler and make hardly any progress.

The regular market as an institution along with its conditions of market like perfect competition and monopoly is absent what comes nearest to it is the weekly market or festival and seasonal meets.

The manufacturer of consumer rather than capital goods is common and the same are consumed, nothing being saved or exchanged in trade.

Specialization based on specially acquired specific technical abilities is absent. However, division of labour based on factors other than specialization, like sex, is widely present.

The notion of property is closely related to display and expenditure of wealth rather than to its accumulation. Material goods, movable and immovable may be referred to as property and this entails the existence of some rules of inheritance. Both types of ownership, collective and individual, are known.

The characteristics of the tribal economy may broadly be viewed in three ways, viz., (i) the structure of the tribal economy, (ii) the tribal economy as a socio-economic and cultural system, and (iii) economic characteristics of the tribal economy.

The structure of the tribal economy is generally based on forest and sea and forest coastal and island tribals. The simple technology and absence of technological aids is the other structural feature of the tribal economy. At the socio-economic and cultural level the family is a unit of both production and consumption. The community itself acts like a co-operative unit, and the tribal communities living in a village or locality are economically independent. The distribution is generally based on gift and ceremonial exchange.

Lastly, in analysing the pure economic characteristics as general economics prescribes, the features are two, viz., absence of profit in economic dealings and presence of periodical markets.

Finally, keeping in view the close association of indigenous tribals production and social organization, a nine point framework has been given to illustrate the fundamental characteristics of tribal economy, (i) Forest-based economy (ii) unit of production, consumption and pattern of labour being the family, (iii) simple technology, (iv) absence of profit in economic dealings, (v) the community, a co-operative unit, (vi) gift and ceremonial exchange (vii) periodical markets, (viii) interdependence, and (ix) the minor institutions related to tribal economy.

Vidyarthi (1977) suggested that the first and foremost characteristics of the tribal economy is the close relationship between their economic life and the natural environment or habitat which is usually the forest. Besides the forest, the existing natural environment moulds their economy to a great extent. For example, at Lakshadweep Islands, the existing ecology of sea and the coconuts forest exert significant influence on the economy of the islanders (Jha, 1992). The

Birhors of Bihar, the Chenchus of Andra Pradesh, the Juangs of Orissa, the Kadars of Kerala, the Paliyans and Panians of Tamil Nadu, etc., depend on the forest and in these areas, the flora and fauna predominates as the primary source of food. The Bhils of western India depend on forest of Mahua and Biri leaves to a great extent. The pastoralist Gaddis of Himachal Pradesh depend on forest for the pasture for *Dhar* for their goats and sheep. In this way, the tribal economy is usually forest-based. However, some changes have occured among the agriculturist tribes like the Mundas, the Oraon, the Santhals, the Raj Gonds, etc., specially after independence of India and their economy is now no more forest-based.

Production and Consumption in Tribal Economy

The family, in the tribal economy is the unit of production. Thus, the mode of production of tribal people is styled "familial" or "domestic". All the members of the family whether husband or wife, parents or children, together form the production unit. The allocation of labour, and decisions for food quests are taken at the family level. They usually produce what they actually need. Yet, it never means that the familial group is self-sufficient. They get the co-operation of individual of other households too. The family is constituted for production by age-groups and is equipped to govern production by possession of the necessary tools which are made indigenously. The children go out in the jungle with their cattle herd and some of them accompany their mother and sister to help in digging out the roots or collection of firewood. Thus, besides the elderly persons the youth form the axis of domestic production. They also take part in their agricultural production, i.e., preparing the fields, sowing, harvesting or in forest operation like collection of minor-forest produce, fishing, hunting, etc.

Thus, the family in a tribal economy plays significant role and is entitled and empowered to act as autonomous unit. In the Birhors, the husband and wife with their children enter the forest in a group. They procure fibres, finish them and then prepare a variety of ropes. All this is done on their own family level. Sometimes they return to their *Tandas* (their house) after two or three days with finished goods and raw materials enough to work for the remaining days of the week.

The pattern of labour in the tribal society is also based on family level. However, in some tribal society, the labour is borrowed from the youth dormatory. For example, among the Muria tribe of Bastar, the youth dormatory is known as *Ghotul* in which the unmarried boys and girls pass their nights and sleep together. During the agricultural operations the members of the entire Ghotul are requisitioned for either agricultural labour or doing some other voluntary works. However, the division of labour is usually sex-wise as women are considered physically weak by the men folk.

So far the consumption is concerned the tribal economy reveals the nature of democratic system at the family level. The forest produce like the roots and fruits, or the hunting games if the animals have been hunted jointly by the clan-men or by the villagers together, those are shared equally. However, the main hunters or the village-chief are given sometimes more shares. But, usually, the democratic pattern of consumption is reflected in the tribal economy.

In the tribal economy, the production and consumption are, more or less, complimentary. The tribal people do not aspire for profit in production. Hence, we find absence of profit in the production of tribal economy. The tribal method of exploitation of nature is crude. It is carried out without any outside efficient technological aid. The impliments and tools are usually indigenously made and are very crude in nature. Thus, the production in the tribal economy is usually based on very simple technology.

Mode of Exchange: Barter and Ceremonial

Exchange is prevalent as a part of economic relationship among the tribals. Gift is given and hospitality is accorded to the social intimates which is an important part of the tribal economy. Herskovits is of opinion that in the tribal society, the production and distribution involve little of the profit, motive, and the labour is only in special instances for higher. The process of distribution in many tribes is, thus, set in a non-economic matrics which takes the form of gifts and ceremonial exchange. Malinowski suggested the mode of

transaction, among the tribe, is based on reciprocity, i.e., material gifts and counter-gifts giving based on social obligation derived typically from kinship relation. The degree of reciprocity is of three kinds, namely:
 (i) General reciprocity,
 (ii) Balanced reciprocity, and
 (iii) Negative reciprocity.

General reciprocity includes in itself the assistance given and taken back or return, sharing hospitality, gifts-taken, mutual aid and generocity. The expectation of reciprocity is left in-definite, unspecified as to qualities, quantity and time. Values of return depends on the donor and the recipient.

Balanced reciprocity is a direct exchange. The return and the goods received should be equal in value. This can be observed at the time of marital transaction between the brides' and grooms' kinship. The barter system of buying or selling is the best example of this degree of reciprocity. This is rather less personal than generalised reciprocity. This does not mean that value of the "give and take" is considered only in money. Social value is also an implied unit.

Negative reciprocity is the attempt to get something for the nothing, e.g., bargaining, higgling, etc.

Malinowski, well-known for his concept of functionalism in anthropological thought (Jha, 1983, 1994), worked among the Trobriand Islanders consisting of four major matrilineal tribes, viz., the Papuan, the Mailu, the Massin and the Pigmy of New-Guinea, wrote elaborately on the *Kula* exchange prevailing among them.

Kula trade is carried on by the tribal communities inhabiting a wide range of islands which form a closed circuit. The articles are of two kinds, which travel constantly in opposite directions. In the direction of the hands of a clock, moves constantly one of these kinds—long necklaces of red shells, called *Soulava*. In the opposite direction or the anti-clockwise moves the other kind of bracelet of white shells known as *Mwali*. Each of these articles, as it travels in its own direction on the closed circuit, meets on the way articles of the other class are constantly being exchanged for them. Every movement of the Kula articles, every details of the transactions, etc., are fixed and regulated by a set of traditional rules and conventions and some acts of the Kula are accompanied by elaborate magical rituals and public ceremonies.

On every island or in a village or more or less, limited number of men take part in the Kula i.e., to receive the goods, hold them for a short time and then pass them on. Therefore, every man who is in the Kula, periodically though not regularly receives one or several *Mwali* or *Soulava* and then has to hand it on to them of his partners, from whom he received the opposite commodity in exchange.

One transaction does not finish the Kula relationship, the rule being *"once in Kula, always in Kula"*, and a partnership beween two men is a permanent and life long affair.

The ceremonial exchange of the two articles is the main and fundamental aspect of the Kula system. We also find a great number of secondary activities and features associated with it. Thus, side by side with the ritual exchange of arm-shells and necklaces, the natives carry on ordinary trade, bartering from one island to another. Kula, thus, is an extremely big and complex institution, both in its geographical extent and in the manifoldness of its components pursuits.

Malinowski has pointed out that not even the most intelligent islander has any clear cut idea of the Kula as a high organised social construction, still less of its sociological function and implication. If one of them is asked that what the Kula is? He would answer his personal experiences and subjective views of the Kula, but nothing approaching the definition. The integral picture does not exist in his mind; he is in it and can not see the whole from the outside.

The Kula is concerned with the exchange of wealth and utilities and, therefore, it is an economic institution.

The Kula is not a super repetitions and precarious form of exchange. It is on the contrary, rooted in myth, backed by traditional law and surrounded with magical rites. All its main transactions are public and ceremonial, which are carried out according to definite rules. Finally, Kula is not done under stress of any need, since its main aim is to exchange articles, which are of no practical use. Myths, magic and traditions have built up around it definite ritual and ceremonial forms.

Among the Indian Tribes, specially among the agriculturist like the Munda, the Oraon, the Gond, etc., the generalised type of reciprocity can clearly be seen at the time of transplanting paddy. The close and distant kins come together to help each other. At the end of the work, the invitees are offered food and drink as hospitality. Wherever *Dhumkuria*, the youth dormatory exists in the Oraon area, the members of the dormatory go for buying musical instruments and other goods. At the time of festival and different auspicious occasion, they pay visit to each other and observe *Mehmani* (being a guest). In the *Ba* festival of the Ho's and the *Bandana* of the Santhals, the people greatly enjoy *Mehmani*. The *Dhumkuria* youths, among the Oraon, have an important role to play in cementing inter-village alliance of friendship. They visit other villages in a group and similarly receive youth from other villages. They exchange greetings, feast and dance together and individual boys enter into ceremonial friendship pacts with the members of Dhumkuria of other village. Gifts are exchanged between friends who form pacts of friendship known as *Sahiya*.

The Bhils of Western India help one another in sowing and harvesting. They borrow cattle on reciprocal basis for ploughing the field.

Balanced reciprocity, i.e., direct exchange, is also prevalent among the tribes on a large scale. The agriculturist tribes like the Oraon, the Munda, the Ho, the Kharia, etc., get their agricultural implements manufactured or repaired by the Lohars, who in returns receive a customary annual payment either in cash or in kind.

The *mirasy* system of the Chenchus of South India can be cited as a long case study to understand the reciprocity. The Chenchus have customary economic collection levied on the pilgrims to the Shrisailam and non-tribal cultivators of land bordering the forest. These customary collections are known among the Chenchus as *mirasy*.

In this way we find that different types of ceremonial exchange and modes of reciprocity are found among the tribes of India and abroad.

Tribal Market and Trade

In addition to the system of exchange and reciprocity, the tribal people have their institution of barter and the tribal political market in their respective areas. Among the tribal regions, we usually don't find permanent markets. These markets—weekly or biweekly or fortnightly or locally known as *Bazar, Hat, Pithia, Shandies,* etc. The tribal villages following in a radius of five to ten km have each a fixed separate weekly market place. In the tribal areas weekly markets play an important market role in the life of tribal people. As a matter of fact, tribal economy is generalised through this tribal market.

The tribal market brings together people from different ethnic groups not only for economic transaction in form of barter or exchanging goods but also for secular and religious activities in the tribal region.

The impact of weekly market on the traditional life too has shown an attitude of accepting innovations. The market is the most powerful channel of communication in the tribal region. Monetary economy has now percolated through the market. Also the weekly market has obtained a place in the social organisation of the tribal people. It has proved for the tribals that the weekly market is the best place of meeting and interacting together. Any announcement of community interest may be broadcast in the tribal market and it will get relayed all over the area immediately. D.P. Sinha (1968) in his study of Tribal market has rightly concluded that this Tribal market maintains a network of socio-cultural ties among the people of its hinterland and gives them a common base for regional ethnology.

Tribal markets also function as an agent of culture change. The tribal market is a centre which brings together a number of communities like, the agriculturist tribes like the Munda, the Oraon, the Gonds, etc; the hunters and the food gatherers like the Birhor, the horticulturists like the Birjia and Kisans; the iron-smelters like the Asurs, the basket makers like the Mahali, and many non-tribals, etc., together. Tribal markets are also places where disputes of tribal villages are discussed and settled. Marriage negotiations are also done in the periodical tribal markets. Of late, the government development agencies have also started to exhibit their development programmes at their weekly tribal market. So, now the tribal market has not only limited its scope to economic transaction and trade by exchange of goods but it is also a centre around which revolves various cultural activities which are linked up with almost every aspect of the tribal way of life.

Primitive Money

Many scholars of primitive economy do not consider the primitive money as money at all. However, some anthropologists have suggested that in most of the tribes of the world some sort of money exist which functions as a medium of exchange both at the inter and intra tribal levels.

The majority of the scholars who have given definitions of primitive money may be classed into two main categories: those who regard money as commodity and those who regard it as an abstract unit. The former category of definition is based on the function of money as a medium of exchange. Its most prominent exponent is Menger who considers primitive money to be virtually synonymous with medium of exchange and rules out any means of payment which does not play that part. Jevons point out that by calling some money and some not, we do not save ourselves from the consideration of their legal economic consideration.

In Locke's words, "money represents a place whereby men were assured of obtaining valuable things equal to those with which they parted". In yet another category of definition stress is laid on the standard of deferred payments and function of money. It is argued that money is the object which is acceptable in the discharge of liabilities.

According to John Stuart Mill, "Money is a medium through which the incomes of different communities are distributed to them and measured by which they estimate their possession."

After these above preliminary conceptions of the primitive money, Pall Einzig suggests a concrete definition of primitive money. He says, "primitive money is an unit or object conforming to a reasonable degree to some standard of uniformities which is employed for reckoning or form making a large proportion of payments customary in the community concerned and which is accepted for payment largely with the intention of employing it for making payment."

Characteristics of Primitive Money

There are various characteristics which are required for a particular object to become a primitive money. According to Jevons a primitive money must fulfil the following criteria, which may be demonstrated through a formula called as CUPDISH.

This formula can be discussed in detail in the following way:
    (a) C stands for cognizability.
    (b) U stands for utility and value.
    (c) P stands for portability.
    (d) D stands for divisibility.
    (e) I stands for indestructability
    (f) S stands for stability of value, and
    (g) H stands for homogeneity.

On the basis of these characteristics a primitive money is determined. A primitive money, therefore, must have the above mentioned qualities and hence any objects fulfilling these criteria will be called a primitive money.

Classification of Primitive Money

The Primitive money may be broadly classified in two groups:
    (i)   Metallic Money, and
    (ii)   Non-Metallic Money.

The non-metallic currencies again may be grouped, according to whether they consist of material produced by the hunting, pastoral, or agricultural or industrial communities. This is the classification adopted by Jevons in his classical chapter on the "Early History of Currency". In hunting communities it consists mostly of the skin of wild animals. In the pastoral communities the skin of domestic animals are used in agricultural groups, the variety of other land products mostly food stuffs are used. In the industrial communities an almost indefinite variety of industrial semi-products like yarn or cloth or finished article such as utensils, weapons and ornaments serve as currencies.

The metallic primitive currencies, too, may be utensils, weapons or ornaments or raw materials, scrap metals and other forms of amorphous choice of metals, which indicates the phase of economic and cultural development of a community.

Origin of Primitive Money

There are many theories of origin of primitive money, some of which are explained below for the benefit of the students.

(1) *The Medium of Exchange Theory:* The medium of exchange theory of the origin of money appears some times in an extreme form which suggests that at a certain moment a deliberate decision to adopt money was made; where the increase in the volume of trade made barter condition intolerable. It is equally important to bear in mind that money was not invented once for all for the entire globe. It is conception implied in Crowther's remark. Schurtz and Thurn Wald are also in favour of this explanation. Hitherto we have been dealing with the origin of money through its function as a medium of exchange.

(2) *Origin through External Trade:* It is a widespread belief that external trade had developed before internal trade. This assumption should not be accepted without close scrutiny; for it has arisen largely through the fact that prehistoric external trade is more easily traced than prehistoric internal trade.

Explorers, early travellers and pioneer traders in their account of economic condition of savage societies give much more information on external trade than on internal trade. This is only natural, since most of these visitors were only interested in their own trade with the natives. On the basis of the assumption the view is taken by many writers that primitive money must have developed primarily from external trade. Bucher is also in favour of this explanation. Relatively scarcity is certainly one of the requirements of money which tends to secure its universal acceptance.

(3) *Origin through Internal Trade:* There is a strong tendency in modern economic literature due to the influence of trade doctrines to underrate the relative importance of home trade compared with foreign trade. Indeed in recent times those engaged professionally in barter transactions were opposed to the introduction of money in African primitive communities. The barter is certainly better placed than the primitive individual for the disposal of goods received in barter. It is possible to imagine, therefore, that in the majority of instances money may have originated through the needs of non-professional trade rather than through professional trade. If we accept this view, then it would appear possible that when money originated through trade it was through home rather than through foreign trade. There are instances in which the purely internal character of the primitive money is quite obvious. Cattle, which is the principal currency of the Ankola of Uganda can only circulate within the tribe.

(4) *The Standard of Value Theory:* Although as a general rule the materialist school supports whole heartedly the medium of exchange theory of the origin of money, a few of its members endorsed the standard of value theory. According to the standard of value theory of the origin of money, it is difficult to see how the medium of exchange could possibly have preceded in archaeological order. The standard of value, considering that the use of a medium of exchange necessary implies the use of a standard of value.

In this theory there is a tendency to fix ratio in particular unit or in several unit convertible to each other on the basis of fixed parties. Menger admits that standard of value may have been employed by primitive communities before the adoption of a medium of exchange.

(5) *The Store of Value Theory:* The part played by the store of value in the origin of primitive money deserves attention. Jevons was among a few economists who realised the full significance of the store of value function of money. Menger admitted that the origin of money must have evolved through hoarding. A detailed explanation of the origin of money through its function as a store of value is provided by Rist who says, "Money has a third function." The practice of

accumulating large stocks of goods serving as a store of value greatly facilitates their acceptability in commercial transaction. This theory is an important theory for the origin of money, due to the fact that it provided the people to store the money for their unimagined future, where there is a great risk of maintaining life and dignities.

(6) *Origin from Standard of Deferred Payment*: Deferred payments played an important part in the life of primitive communities from a very early stage. Deferred deliveries due to national conditions, sowing seeds was often lent in agricultural communities and, was repayable out of the next crop. Blacksmith and other artisans were paid often during harvest. Such theoretical confirmation of the possibility that money has originated through it's use as a standard of deferred payment has been provided by Hawstrey, Tylor & Ellis etc.

(7) *Origin through Ornamental and Ceremonial Function*: Ornamental requirements must have played a very important part in the origin of money. Indeed there is reason to believe that shells which were the earliest currencies in many parts of the world, served as ornaments before they were put to monetary use. Shell must first have been used or valued because of their ornamental use, and their comparative durability and uniformity made them suitable subsequently to undertake monetary function. So the claim of the theory of ornamental origin of money is evidently a strong one.

(8) *Religious Origin*: The religious aspect of money may be concluded under the following headings:-

(i) Money may have originated in many instances through regular requirements for specific standardized objects for the purposes of sacrifices to deities.

(ii) In many communities the creation of money is attributed to supernatural power.

(iii) Magic qualities attributed to certain objects have led to their adoption for monetary use.

(iv) The fixing of fines for breaking taboos and fees for performances of religious rites gave rise to the need for a standardised unit.

Laum's theory about the origin of money through religious sacrifices came as a reaction against the materialistic conception. The evolution of economic system in general was itself eagerly influenced by the religious factor. According to Edward Hahn, the evolution of pastrol economy, for instance, was largely due to sacrificial requirement. Laum has evolved the theory that the practice of making sacrifice to deity was to a large extent a form of barter between man and his gods. The fact that money is believed to be of divine origin.

(9) *Political Origin of Primitive Money*: Political payment during the early phases of civilization may have assumed the following forms:
  (i) Payment to the political authority,
  (ii) Payment by the political authority to the service men.
  (iii) Payment between members of the tribe or between members of different tribes, regulated by the political authorities. In the south west Africa the Bergdama paid over a period annual tribute to the Saan in the form of *dagga* category of intoxicating herbs.

(10) *Matrimonial Origin of Primitive Money:* It is also necessary to consider the possibility of its origin and development from the primitive form of marriage. Payment of bride money was also influenced by questions of prestige. Bride money came to occupy such an important place in primitive social system. In Africa, in Pacific Island, or among the Latin American Indians and Central Asiatic Nomads, youngmen waiting to marry, had to earn money in order to be able to buy their bride as a general rule. Only highly valued objects were accepted as bride money. Cattle, of course, was favourite bride money among many pastoral tribes. So it is believed by a number of ethnologists that money originated through matrimonial form of payment.

CHAPTER VI

Political Anthropology

Meaning and Concept

In social anthropology the political life of the tribals reflects a paradoxical situation between the democracy and the monarchy. A tribal leader, either democratically elected or through hereditary rule, governs the community and their political activities. The traditional tribal panchayat or the modern elected body, the organisation of their government, tribal law and justice, etc., are briefly the subject of the political anthropology.

Tribal political associations are of various types and incorporate individuals elders, families, a clan group, a village and a tribal territory. Although a tribal territory is considered by the tribal people at par with the stateless government, still they are micro-political in nature. Thus the simple tribal communities have their own political influences which may spread quite beyond the limit of the small territory. The political characteristics of tribals may broadly be looked at through their social organisation. They are: (i) political association based on their clan/lineage; (ii) political association based on the village; and (iii) political association of a group of villagers or territory.

The first and foremost characteristic of the clan is lineage; clanship is politically more significant. The living groups of clansmen claim to know with some certainty the genealogical links between themselves and the founding ancestor. Here the clan has a systematic genealogical structure, with numerous branches called "lineages". These lineages stand in known genealogical relationship to one another.

Tribes and their sections, then, are the political communities composed of groups of people of different lines of ancestry occupying a common territory. Clans and their lineages are the descent groups of people claiming common ancestry which individual members often are territorially widely scattered. In some cases clansmen may have only the knowledge of their origin about the clan-founder. There are tribes like the Oraons which include groups of clansmen from quite different clans, and where strict rules against marrying within one's own clan ensure that marital alliances are formed only with unrelated people. One clan may then be recognized as having priority in the whole tribal territory, and those living within that territory and who are not members of that clan, will have to explain their presence by their relationship to the original settlers. The branches of a "dominant clan" of this type spread throughout the territorial sections of the tribe and others who live in those sections identify themselves politically with their own lineage of the dominant clan even though they do not belong to it by descent.

Lineage segmentation is particularly important as a principle of political structure where central authority is weak or unknown and where, therefore, lineage members have to provide their own security against others of the same tribe, as well as against outsiders. The Oraon's lineage is locally known as *Khunt*. A lineage is further divided into a number of families. All the members of a family are governed by the father. The head of the *Khunt* is generally the eldest man of the lineage who functions as its political head. The members of a lineage group of the Gonds observe rites in common. In each lineage there is a specialist who recollects the genealogy of a member which proves to be a uniting and inspiring factor for the person concerned. A lineage also functions as a group at times. The Bhils lineage is structured with a depth of five or six generations and on occasions they function as one unit. Among the Purums, a Kuki tribe, the members of a sub-sib regard themselves as related and a number of families are, thus, united.

Further, the political field extends to the village itself. The tribal village works actively as a political unit. To our conception the village, village officer and village administration in areas regulate and work for the tribal.

This mechanism functions and its officers are known by different designations among the various tribes. In the minor tribes like the Birhor, Juang, etc., the ordering of the social, political and ritual relations of the village is in the hands of one man. The Malers and the Kamars have *Manjhi* and the *Baiga* as their respective heads. But among major tribes like the Santhal, Bhil, Munda, etc., we find a differentiation of function and authority vested in two headmen, each with his own field of interest and prescribed duties. A primary differentiation of function splits village affairs into secular and sacerdotal spheres of activity with a headman responsible for each. Among some tribes, this differentiation is further emphasized by the appointment of assistants to help each headman in the discharge of his duties.

Most of the tribes have a judicial machinery to deal with disputes, breaches of peace and social offences at the village level. In this way, we find that the political anthropology deals with a very wide canvas of the political behaviour of the primitive people and all these components of the political behaviour fall within the meaning and scope of this chapter.

Definition of Primitive Law

Various definitions have been given by different authors. Some of which are quoted precisely below for the benefit of the students.

According to Radcliffe Brown 'Political organisation is that aspect of the total organisation, which is concerned with the control and regulation of the use of physical force."

Hobel says, "a law is a social norm, the infraction of which is sanctioned in thread or in fact by the application of physical force by a party possessing the socially recognised privilege of so acting."

According to Cardozo "Law is a principle, rule of conduct, so established as to justify a prediction with reasonable certainty that will be enforced by courts if its authority is challenged."

Majumdar and Madan are of opinion that, "Law consists of a set of principles which permit the use of force to maintain political and social organization within a territory."

R. H. Lowie, the famous American anthropologist, was of opinion that the early primitive law was conceived largely in kinship rather than in territorial terms. It coincides more closely with the ethical notions, hence the public opinion of the people in question, it fails to discriminate public and private wrongs, the crimes and torts of our modern jurisprudence. It has been further argued that in primitive societies the growth of law is a slow and spontaneous process of usages and customs being given the sanction of time and force. There is no legislation or the written law in the sense we know it in our civilized societies. There is no sustained conscious and deliberate attempt at making or modifying the tribal laws. These are some of basic nature and characteristics of primitive law. I now discuss it with the special reference to the Indian tribes:

1. Tribal law is based on clans/phratry-organisation.,
2. It has territorial limitation.
3. It is based on customary law and usages.
4. A strong sense of collectivism prevails in the primitive law.
5. The oath and ordeals are main mode of evidence in tribal law.
6. Punishment is awarded in the shape of fine, compensation to the aggrieved party; communal feasts, and *Puja* (worship) to the village deity, etc.
7. Breach of law is taken as to affect not only to an individual but to the whole tribal society.

Difference between custom and law

There are many differences between custom and law, some of which are given below:

1. Primitive law originated with the origin of stateless primitive govt, while the primitive custom originated slow and automatically
2. Primitive law is imposed on the society from outside but customs originate from within the society.

3. Primitive law is backed by the so-called stateless government, while customs are backed by the traditions and faiths.
4. Thus, customs are sustained by common acceptance. Customs are the most spontaneous of all social rules and often the most compelling.

The primitive law evidences are usually based on the oath and ordeals. As referred to above, collective responsibility is one of the important criteria of the primitive law.

Social Sanction in Primitive Law

The primitive law is an unwritten law which has been sanctioned through local custom and traditions which are transmitted orally from generations to generations. Thus, primitive law is backed by customs and traditions and its social sanction is related not only to religious practices and usages but also to jurisprudence, philosophy and various other local traditions.

Out of all these socio-religious phenomena, primitive jurisprudence relating to the formal or informal legal structures of primitive law has not been studied in detail, neither it is taught in detail and hence for the benefit of students, I give below some of the salient features of the primitive jurisprudence.

Anthropological studies relating to jurisprudence consider the formal structures of primitive legal system, legal status, legal professionals, and legal institutions, in contrast to the ways in which law in actually applied and enforced at the local level. Anthropologists are particularly interested in the low-level (micro-level) perspective because it affords first hand evidence for comparison of values and ideals within the written or at least formal word of the law, as well as practical application of those values in the daily lives of specific groups of people. Such anthropological studies include ways in which legal concepts and definitions vary between different societies and sub-cultures, the ways in which rules and law are interpreted and applied differently in various segments of society, and the consequence of this type of real and ideal structure in legal system of the management of conflict, change, and development within a society.

Comparison involves not only the study of concepts and practices which differ between whole societies (e.g., American versus Polynesian legal values) but also the analysis of various aspects and levels of one legal system within the same society.

When several legal systems coexist within the same political unit, the situation is called legal pluralism. Legal systems change internally because of the ways people use them, but they can also change when different principles and procedures are introduced from external sources. The application of British rule of law to indigenous African populations during the colonial period is a good example of this type of legal change.

The comparative study of changing legal systems and the consequences of planned programs of "development" for unwesternized legal systems also fall within the comparative scope of cross-cultural jurisprudence in anthropology.

Scholars whose works have become classics in the anthropological study of comparative jurisprudence include Sir Henry Maine (Ancient Law, 1861), Montesquien De l' Esprit Des Lois, (1950), and E.A. Hoebel (The Law of Primitive Man, 1954).

In brief, from the point of view of legal sanction behind the primitive law scholars have made two broad typologies, viz., (a) positive sanction and (b) negative sanction. In the primitive law positive sanctions are based on commonly approved customs and traditions which have integrative factors to bind together the clansmen or the villagers or the members of the tribal society inhabiting the whole territory. For instance, the totemic insignia are commonly honoured and respected; totemic exogamy is also commonly approved and sanctioned by the societies, the breach of which is considered the breach of law. Thus, there are the positive sanctions of the primitive law. So far as the negative sanctions are concerned, there are negative, destructive and disintegrating factors prevailing in the society. For instance, if someone breaks the incest-taboo, or someone breaks the clan exogamy rule, dishonour the totemic emblems, etc., under these circumstances, the council of elders fails to stop these activities, we call negative sanctions. There are chances for breaking the positive sanctions in the societies. Thus, in the primitive law it has been found that steps are usually taken to provide the kind of institutional and inspirational continuity for the preservation of positive sanction in the affairs of tribal law and thus, it creates a feeling of solidarity, which unites the members of the tribal group.

Structure of the Primitive Government in Tribal Societies

The political structure on which the primitive government and the political machinery rest is of great significance for the students of social anthropology. The tribal political pattern may also be viewed along with their political institution. Besides certain individuals, the political institutions also exercised the political control over the members of the community. The political field of activities in the tribal societies may be broadly divided into two groups with many further sub-types: (a) traditional political field, and (b) contemporary political field.

The first type is the product of their traditional political life where political affairs are combined with social and religious affair. The second type has emerged out of culture-changes, culture-contact, the mode of electing the village chief under the existing democratic set up.

The verdict of the tribal panchayat or the headman of the village is law to the tribal people. The sanction behind it is the great faith in the elders and the village leadership. Every tribal village has some type of political machinery to look after the village affairs.

As mentioned above, the traditional political field of the tribals is confined to the council of village elders, or village headmen, village panchayat, and so on. All these institutions consisting of a single person or a group of persons have inter-related, cross-cutting fields where sometimes one surpasses the other varying from situation to situation. The structure of the traditional political institutions are mainly of the following kinds.

    (i) The council of elders is a temporary body of selected villagers, generally consisted of clan-elders to look into cases brought before them,

(ii) The village headman usually works on a hereditary post and or subject to villagers' opinion, if and when required,

(iii) The village-panchayat: a body of the village councils headed by a village headman. The members of the village council may by directly elected by the villagers or nominated by the village headman,

(iv) The union of villages or a regional panchayat is headed by the regional head as prevalent among the Mundas of Chotanagpur where *Parha* system is still prevailing and the head of the *Parha* is known as the *Parha Chief*,

(v) And, finally the tribal chief is also a hereditary post of supreme judicial authority at the tribal level. For example, the *Chharidar* is considered to be the tribal chief of the Ollar Gadba tribe.

The character of the contemporary political field is growing up fast and is replacing the traditional political set up of the tribes at the global level to a great extent.

When we look at the history of breaking up traditional political institution in India, we have to go back when the Moghul Emperor granted the right of *Diwani* to the East-India Company in 1765. In Central India, they made continous efforts to get full authority over the *Mankis* of the Mundas and as such control over the tribal villages. The village communities and councils were disrupted and that's why the frustrated people chose the way of rebellion several times. In India the traditional political situation once again received a jolt when Christian missionaries entered the tribal areas. Apart from their religious aims and reform movements the missionaries started taking part in village affairs. Taken together, the British policy of land rent system, introduction of middlemen, police and judicial arrangements in the tribal areas and consequently launching of different religious aggrarian and political movements by the tribals and their leaders, policy of extreme type of isolation in certain tribal pockets in the name of peace and protection, the new democratic set-up in the Republic of India, expansion of educational and developmental programmes, etc., gave birth to contemporary political systems of the tribals. In this way the powers of the tribal village council and village head were slowly reduced due to emergence of the democratice forces all over India.

Difference between State and Stateless Political System

There are some basic differences between the laws practiced by the modern government and the laws and customs practiced by the stateless government. As referred to earlier, the tribal societies have a type of government where laws are not written, rather those are based on oral transmissions of traditions and custom. However, precisely we may point out that in a stateless government like the tribals, a sense of collective responsibilities override the individuals' right and priviledges. Again, in a stateless society, the mode of punishment is deterrent which may be awarded not only to an individual but to any kinsman of the accused, which is not relevant, neither desirable in the rule of the modern government. Further, in a stateless government, evidences are based not only on the presence of witnesses but on the mode of oath and ordeals which are in vogue in the concerned societies, and these are not the relevant matters of evidences in the modern system of government where physical presence of witnesses and their cross-examinations are the basic sources of evidences. Thus, in the tribal societies, what anthropologists call a stateless government, the primitive law is basically based on the perpetuation of magic and religion, while in the modern government law is based on scientific and logical explanations. The early writers of primitive law like Maine in his book, "*Ancient Law*", (1861) stated, "the enquiries of the jurists are in truth prosecuted much as enquiry into physics and physiology was prosecuted before observation had taken the place of assumption, theories plausible and comprehensive but absolutely unverified such as the law of nature or the social compact, enjoy a universal preference over sober research into the primitive history of society and law."

Philosophical speculations are of no use in the modern state government while it is of great value in the tribal society, although most of the times philosophical speculations are unsupported by factual evidence.

Finally, it may be concluded that while in a stateless government the elementary state of primitive law is intimately bound up with magic and religion and legal sanctions are closely related to ritual sanctions, while in the law of modern state, magic and religion find no place. The social anthropologists, therefore, emphasized that a full understanding of the complexities of law in simpler societies can be made only by a comparative study of whole systems of social sanctions.

Justice and Punishment in Primitive Societies

Most of the tribes have a judicial machinery to deal with disputes, breaches of peace and social offences at the village level as well as at the community level. However, it is usually a village council or assembly of elders known as panchayat where decisions are taken and punishments are awarded.

In Indian tribal situations, where some tribes and their settlement are so small, that they do not have any organisation at the village level. For example, among the Malers (Vidyarthi, 1963), the councils of elders of the village is presided over by the *Manjhi* and the *Gorait* acts as the public prosecutor. The panchayat is called at the instance of the Manjhi by the Gorait. Among the tribes of Central India, viz., the Mundas, the Santhals, the Ho's, the Oraons, the Gonds, etc., each village has a panchayat. Sexual offences among them are dealt with the clan elders. In villages having only one clan, the clan elders coincide with the village elders. In a village consisting of many clans, the population of several villages would be organised into clan units for purposes of trial of sexual offences.

Various cases of offences like repudiation of debt, adultery, theft or wilful destruction of others property, witchcraft and sorcery, etc., are usually dealt with at the village level council. However, in cases of disapproval or in the cases of inter-village disputes, the authorities of the community level are informed and invited by the village leaders to settle the dispute. Thus, the political association to settle the dispute and award the punishment in cases of inter-village differences, etc., are taken at the highest level known as territorial leadership. For example, the *Paraha Raja* heads the *Paraha,* a union of a number of Oraon villages, whereas *Manki* heads a Ho *Pirh* (regional panchayat of the Hos). The Pargana of Gonds, a union of villages is headed by Deshmukh or Patel or by Pargana Manjhi under which, there are 10 to 12 villages. Inter-village disputes are usually settled by the head of the union of villages as referred to above.

As mentioned earlier, the evidences called for while deciding a criminal case is of two kinds—Oath, Ordeal.

In cases of taking oath, a person concerned has to come before a council of village elders who will prescribe the nature of oath. It is believed that whatever the person says is the truth. If he tells a lie the anger of god or goddesses will destroy or punish him. As for the form of oath, it varies from tribe to tribe. For example, among the Malers, an accused is brought before the *Jhanda Gossaiya* and is asked to touch a knife placed at the sacred centre and while touching the knife, he is asked to say—"I will die if I will tell a lie" and, thereafter, he narrates the incident in detail. However, among the Hos an oath is taken in the name of *Singa Bonga* or *Hatu Bonga*. The Santhals utter—"Dharam Dharam" before they narrate the incident.

Sometimes the offender is subjected to some torture before the declaration of the verdict of the panchayat. If the person escapes without injury, he is supposed to be non-guilty. In some cases, for example, the accused is asked to lick salt or fire. If he suffers an injury he is believed to have committed the said crime. This is common with the tribes all over India. The force behind this type of treatment is the strong belief in the sacred spirit of the unknown world. They take it as guaranteed that god or the supreme being is the greatest judge.

The oath and the ordeal serve as a means of voluntary submission of the accused to law. It is obeyed mainly because of the fear of the anger of the supreme being.

The punishment awarded to the accused is generally a fine in cash or kind or both depending upon the seriousness of the crime and the capability of the person concerned. The fine is usually spent in giving a communal feast or as an offering to the supernatural power for appeasing them. The most serious punishment among the Santhal is *Bitlaha* which follows the sentence of formal excommunication from the tribe.

The concept behind punishment among the tribal societies is also remarkable. The tribal societies believe that the punishments should be such to compensate the aggrieved, to purify the offenders and to re-admit the guilty person after paying a fine or after throwing a feast.

In brief, it may be concluded that the tribal political life is characterised by the following important features:
- (a) Tribal law depends on the agnatic relation like the clan and lineage.
- (b) The group relation and territorial relations take part in political affairs.
- (c) The tribal laws have their origin in social custom and tradition
- (d) The tribal laws do not make any distinction between public and private crime and all matters of social relations and disputes are brought before the village council for trial.
- (e) Oath and ordeals are modes of evidence.
- (f) Punishment is awarded in the shape of fine, compensation to the aggrieved, offer of communal feasts and offering to the supremebeing.
- (g) A breach of norm is likely to affect the whole society, they believe.
- (h) It is also believed that the punishment, awarded to the accused by the village council, has also been given by the supernatural power.

All these characteristics of the tribal law go a long way to form the axis on which the entire political life of the tribal society rests.

Nation Building Process in a State

Nation building is a process through which a country achieves a mature level of political status so that it becomes a committed state to uphold the welfare of its citizens, and effective government in charge of the integrity of the boundary of the nation and a responsible member of the world community of the nations.

Thus, this is a process of refinement in the life of a nation to fulfil the growing aspirations of her citizens as well as to play a constructive political role at the global level. Thus, it's a process which has been strengthened specially after the Second World War. A new process of nation building started taking place only a couple of years back in the then U.S.S.R., which has split now into several nations and the aspirations for enjoying the democratic life are still emerging for the citizens in the newly formed countries.

Nation building process is based mainly on the following main factors.

(1) Economic Factor in Nation Building

This is the most important point through which the economic development of a nation is made and the welfare measures of the citizen are achieved.

(ii) Modern Theory of Nation Building

In the nation building process, the political scientists have suggested many modern theories on the basis of which constitutions have been written differently in different countries. That's why, sometimes confusions arise and differences occur over the implementation of a particular ideology for the welfare of the citizens of the world.

(iii) Political dimension of the Nation Building

At the global level, we find different types of government like the democratically elected body of the government, the presidential form of government, the kingship, etc., and therefore, the mode of development and welfare programmes or the areas of priority of development vary from country to country. However, one common thing in the nation building process is to protect the national sovereignty and integrity of nation and to gear the machinery of development for the benefit of the citizens of the country.

The scholars of political science, interested in the study of the nation building process, suggest many theories, viz., the general theory of nation building process, the periphery theory of nation-building, the need of new theory of nation building, specially for the new emerging nation and in this way, this subject is attracting the attentions of scholars from different subjects, and hence, a multi-disciplinary approach has been suggested.

Chapter VII

Anthropology of Religion

Meaning and Scope

The word, *religion* has been derived from the root word *religio*, which means "to bind together" and religion actually does it. Religion has exercised the most profound influence over man's thoughts since time immemorial. Even today, when man has made tremendous progress specially in the field of science and technology, he is utterly restless in his quest for some unseen powers which may give him some inspiration and solace. It is this quest for the supreme knowledge, which is beyond the human ommissions and commissions and which yet shapes his destiny in the world. It is probably the main cause, which has given rise to some kind of religion in all societies.

In social anthropology, however, we give more emphasis on the study of tribal religion and, therefore, we will discuss below some of the salient features of the primitive religion for the benefit of the student.

The usual way of looking at religion is to regard it as bodies of erroneous belief's and illusory practices. There is no doubt that the history of religion has been a great part of a history of error and illusions. In all ages men hope that by the proper performance of religious actions or observances, they would obtain some specific benefit: health, long life, children, material well being, success in hunting, rain, good crops, victory in war, etc.

There is another way in which we may approach the study of religion. We may argue that any religion is an important or essential part of the social machinery as are morality and law, part of the complex system by which human beings are enabled to live together in an orderly arrangement of social relations. From this point of view religion is dealt with out from the point of view of its origin but from the point of view of social functions of a religion, as Durkheim, (1912), Radcliffe Brown (1964) and others emphasised. Thus, the meaning and scope of religion has been interpreted from different angles by different scholars. While E.B. Taylor laid emphasis on the origin of religion from the evolutionary point of view as did James Frazer in his classical work *Golden Bough* (in 12 volumes), Malinowski and Radcliffe Brown gave the functional interpretation of religion. Radcliffe Brown was of opinion that in attempting to understand a religion, emphasis should be given on the study of rites rather than on the beliefs. The same view has been expressed by Loisy, who justifies his selection of sacrificial rites as the subject of his analysis of religion, and further argued that rites are in all religions the most stable and lasting element.

The great pioneer of the science of religion, Robertson Smith says, "a connection with every religion whether ancient or modern we find, on the one hand, certain belief's sand, on the other, certain institutions, ritual practices and rules of conduct. Our modern habit is to look at religion from the side of belief rather than that of practices"(1907).

The savage religion can stand as representing natural phenomena and its complexities in detail. It is believed that the moral government of the universe is an essential tenet of natural religion (or primitive religion). Primitive animism, what the tribal religion is usually addressed to, is almost devoid of that ethical element which to the educated modern mind is the main-spring of practical religion. Ethical laws in the tribal society stand on their own ground of tradition and public opinion, comparatively independent of the animistic beliefs and rites.

The rite of ancestor-worship is an important practice in the perpertuation of tribal religion. Tylor's interpretation of primitive religion which he called animism, as this word has been derived from the word *anima* which means *soul*, is entirely based on ancestor-worship. R.R. Marett in his book

"The Threshold of Religion" (1909), however, differs from his teacher Tylor and suggested that instead of soul, "it is the "nature" which guides the destiny of the primitive people" and he, therefore, coined the word *animatism* for understanding the primitive religion.

Under this background of the meaning and interpretations of religion, we now give the various definitions of religion precisely.

Definitions of Primitive Religion

No single definition of religion is universally accepted. Value judgement, historical stereotypes and immense cultural variety cause disagreement about the nature and range of the phenomena involved. Anthropologists have tended to broaden the term minimal definition of Tylor (1874: 424-425), "a belief in spiritual beings", to the carefully explicit definition of Geertz (1966:4) "a system of symbols which acts to establish powerful, pervasive and long-lasting moods and motivations in men by formulating conceptions of a general order of existence and clothing these conceptions with an aura of facility that the moods and motivations seem uniquely realistic".

Most anthropologists stress the institutionalized interaction with super human beings or extraordinary powers capable of harming or aiding humans. Religion is firmly regarded as a cultural institution distinguishable from others by its "culturally patterned interaction with culturally postulated super human beings" (Spiro 1966:96). Both psychological and sociological factors are required to describe the role and function of a particular religion in the lives of individuals and their society. Beliefs and practices are so organized as to "shape an ethic manifest in the behaviour" (Birnbaum (1964:588) and characterize each religious system.

If all religions involve belief in some spiritual beings, then the ordering of these beliefs into a structure and hierarchy differs greatly according to the religious system. So-called Great religions such as Islam and Christianity depend on a prophet (Mohammed) or Messiah (Jesus) who reveals the word of a unique creator (trinitarian godhead for the Christians). Classcial Greek and Roman religions packed their pantheons with defined culture heroes. Many modern religions immortalize their supreme leaders as divinities (the Japanese Emperor, the Tibetan Dalai Lama, the Nilotic Shilluk king, the Ismaile Aga Khan). Monotheistic Christanity and unorthodox Islam both produce saints who acts as patrons channeling belief and ritual. Manifestations of gods and holy personages (love, the Virgin Mary) focus tribal and cult as do the *avatars* of polytheistic Hinduism (Vishnu, Shiva). The anthropopsychic conception of spiritual beings is variously capricious, bengeful and ethical but all are the sources of supernatural power whether personal (grace) or impersonal (*mana* in polynesia and its equivalents elsewhere).

Socialization of an orthodoxy in literate societies led to Great Traditions perpetuated by sacred texts (Koran, Bible, Puranas, etc.) and formal ritual directed by a public functionary—priesthood. Temple, Mosque, and Church epitomize the institutionalization of religion.

Rituals are regarded as the dogmatic and socially sanctioned representations of myths. Calendrical rites publicly mark the passage from one season to anothers (e.g., the first fruits or harvest festivals) and are usually performed for the commonwealth; critical rites mark the passage from one individual human condition to another (hence rites-de-passage such as initiation rites.) The Durkheimian sacred/secular dichotomy, which distinguishes (by the element of mysticism) ritual from ceremony, marks a clear cut line between religious and magical acts. For Leach (1954:13) ritual is the symbolically significant aspect of routine. In the modern West, secularization and the declining influence of institutionalized religion have been accompanied by a rise of the occult wherein symbolic behaviour and rituals, merge the sacred (religious) and profane (technological).

In this way, we find that many definitions of religions have been provided by different scholars and various interpretations have been given since the days of Tylor and Durkheim. The modern anthropologists like Evans-Pritchard holds that the main objectivity in the studies of religions required that we build up general conclusions from particular ones. This view helps us to an extent in fixing up an objective definition of religion. He tells us that one must not ask what is religion, but what are the main features of such a religion. In this connection I feel that this may be good for a strategy but it does not seem practicable. For, unless one knows extensively what religion is, how can an anthropologist explain it?

Trying to fix up a definition of religion, Melford E. Spiro (1968) suggests that the term applies, of course, that what ever phenomena we might wish to designate by religion, religion is an attribute of social groups comprising a component part of their cultural heritage. And "that its component features are acquired by means of the same inculturation, processes as the other variables of a cultural heritage are acquired" (1968). He further adds that this means that the variables constituting a religious system have the same ontological status as those of other cultural system. If beliefs are normative, its rituals are collective and its values are prescriptive, Spiro added. This is nearer, as he himself argues, to Durkheim's principle that there can be religion without a Church.

Religion and supernaturalism are also closely interrelated. Similarly religion and philosophy, on one hand, and religion and ethics, on the other hand, are also intimately related. Study of all these aspects of religion provide a very vast scope and meaning of religion in social anthropology:

Theory of Religion

A.Van Gennep (1908) classified the religion in his book *Rites of Passage* in the following way:

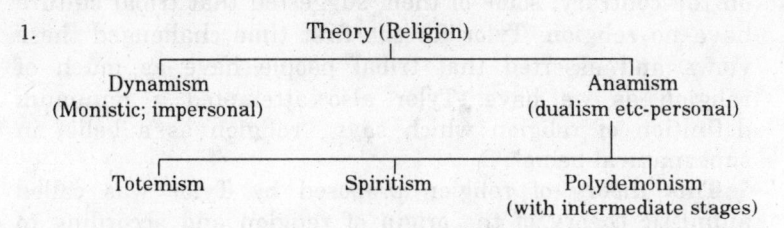

1.
               Theory (Religion)
      ┌─────────────────┴─────────────────┐
    Dynamism   Anamism
(Monistic; impersonal)   (dualism etc-personal)

┌──────────────┬──────────────┐
Totemism   Spiritism   Polydemonism
                                    (with intermediate stages)

A. Van Gennep gave theory of religion in a tabular form. However, James Frazer gave the technique of religion (magical rites) in the following form:

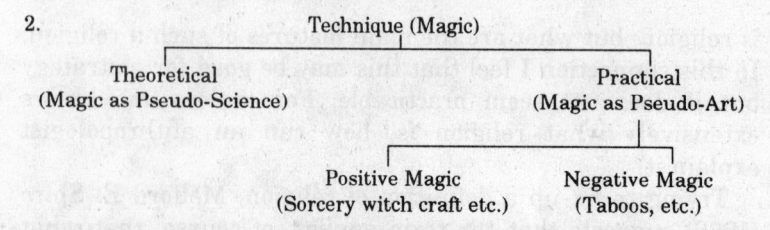

2.
```
                    Technique (Magic)
        ┌──────────────────┴──────────────────┐
     Theoretical                           Practical
(Magic as Pseudo-Science)            (Magic as Pseudo-Art)
                            ┌──────────────────┴──────────────────┐
                      Positive Magic                        Negative Magic
                 (Sorcery witch craft etc.)                  (Taboos, etc.)
```

On the basis of these typologies of the theory and techniques (magical rites), a number of theoretical concepts developed in the study of religion which may be summarised below:

Tylor's Theory of Animism

Religion is universal but it is not universally the same. In a particular tribe, there may be only a couple of ghosts or spirits to guide the destiny of man but in an another tribal group, there may be a full pantheon of ghosts and spirits. Thus, the concept of *soul* (or *anima* as proposed by Tylor) may vary from tribe to tribe. However, it is universally accepted that the ancestor-worship as prevalent among the primitive societies implies the idea of spirit. The people all over the world believe in some kind of existence and, thus, the idea of soul develops, which is supposed to be essentially non-material. This belief in sprits is known as *animism*.

By the time Tylor has started writing on religion, it was thought that tribal people have no religion. The travellers, missionaries and traders have brought narrative stories of primitive people which nowhere mentioned religion. However, on the contrary, some of them suggested that tribal culture have no religion. Tylor for the first time challenged these views and asserted that tribal people have as much of religion as we have. Tylor also attempted a minimum definition of religion which says, "religion as a belief in supernatural being".

This theory of religion proposed by Tylor was called animistic theory of the origin of religion and according to Tylor religion and animism were thought as synonyms to each other.

In fact, animism is the ground work of the philosophy of

religion which Tylor described in detail in his classical book *Primitive Culture* (1871). In the beginning it was thought that this is barely a meagre definition of religion but as a matter of fact Tylor gave a currency to the term animism and to the whole animistic theory of religion.

Tylor regarded, as per the above discussion, animism as a form of religion, but the latter writers have tried to differentiate between the two. R.H. Lowie in his book *Primitive Religion* (1925) argues that animism and religion largely overlap and they are not identical. He further says that supernatural powers need not necessarily be the shadow of souls. Lowie further criticises Tylor who fails to explain as to why the dualism of the soul and body does not exclude a profound unity and an intimate interpretation of the two. However, at another place Lowie admits that Tylor's theory of animism is avowedly a physiological interpretation, pure and simple. It lacks the empirical observation, Lowie added.

Max Muller's Theory of Naturalism

An important theory that was proposed later to explain the religious phenomena developed by Max Muller is now known as *naturalism*. The animistic theory gives primacy to the worship of the soul and derives the worship of nature from it. But the German scholar, Max Muller, and a great Indologist, reverses the order and derives the belief in the supernatural being from the sensation aroused in man by the overwhelming and at times cataclymic manifestations of nature. MaxMuller suggested that man first called the striking phenomena of nature by terms which denoted their activities— "a thunder bolt was called something that tears of the soil or that spread fire, the mind something signs and whistles, and so on". Thus, the primitive man was inspired by the natural phenomena and he sought to explain it. This description of the phenomena of nature in term of human or quasi-human activities led to their interpretation in anthropomophic terms, and divine personality were invented to account for the activities of natural phenomena. The origin of religion, thus, according to Max-Muller lies in a body of thought and language, since the words used to describe the inspiring phenomena of nature denoting human activities. In this connection it may be noted that some religions of world are nearer to naturalism. For example, the Aryan religion, expressed in the Vedic literature, has elements parallel to naturalism.

The Theory of Manaism

Codrington is said to have coined the term *Mana*, a special form of animist theory which he called *manaism*. While working among the Melanesians, Codrington borrowed the word *mana* to designate this force. It may designate a type of supernatural power in a person or in an object and such a set of beliefs was called *mana* as used by the Melanesians. Majumdar's description, analysis of the conception of *Bonga* among the Ho (a tribe of Chotanagpur) falls in line with Codrington's theory of primitive religion. Some North American tribe call this power as *Orenda*.

This explanation of the origin of religion is opened to the main criticism, to some extent, level against Tylor.

Functional Theory of Religion

Besides Durkheim, Malinowski and Radcliffe Brown have proposed the functional explanation of primitive religion. Malinowski, while working among the Trobriand Islanders, discovered that religion is intimately connected with various emotional stages, which are stages of tensions. Their magical and religious practices move around the fishing expeditions. These are the stages of fear when disaster may occur in the sea and it may give rise to different types of tensions. In order to control this emotionally upset state of existence, religion is made use of as a tool of adaptation to get rid of stress and strain. In other words, religion has a function of bringing about a readjustment between man and supernatural forces. It is a device to secure success, mental and physical stability in an individual's life.

In the functional analysis of religion, Radcliffe Brown takes a little different stand. He says that the function of religion is not to purge fear and other emotional, strain from the human mind, but to instil a sense of dependence in it. He says that, ultimately, the survival of the group is more important than that of the individual, because without social survival, individual survival is not possible. According to Radcliffe Brown adherence to a norm of behaviour is essential in terms of social survival and it is the fear of supernatural control and punishment as also the anticipation of support in the case of socially approved conduct, that brings about adherence. Therefore, according to Radcliffe Brown, the function of religion is to create a twofold feeling of dependence on society and thereby obtain the individual's concurrence with the social norms, the ultimate aim being social survival. In this way, Radcliffe Brown laid emphasis on the function of religion to perpetuate the social survival of the society.

Radcliffe Brown and Malinowski took inspiration from the writings of Emile Durkheim. Thus, the sociological explanations given by Radcliffe Brown and Malinowski are derived in part from Durkheim's theory of religion. Durkheim was of opinion (1912) that "religion is what religion does". Durkheim's religion's notions are born and conceived of the findings of social group collecting together for festival and other social gatherings. Social life on such occasions impressess the human-mind. Thus, Durkheim defines religion with regard to the part of which it is composed. These parts are beliefs and rites. The beliefs constitute the static part of religion, and rites are the dynamic part of religion. More and more beliefs constitute theology and a type of transcendentalism occurs in religion.

Durkheim's Concept of Sacred and Profane

Durkheim in his famous book *Elementary Form of Religious Life* (1912) used two important concepts, viz, *sacred* and *profane*, which are still used all over the world in the study of primitive religion. In every tribe, there is some sort of distinction, which is made between *sacred* and profane. Durkheim suggested that the sacred consists of, which he termed religions and the profane consists of magic or the pseudo-science. Durkheim was of opinion that in religion we have only sacred beliefs; beliefs which referred to God and deities who are actually symbolic of society. However, profane beliefs and practices are not sacred and do not form part of religion.

The word, "sacred", has been derived from the French word *Sacrres* which means pure with religious sanctity. The word profane means forbidden. While studying the tribes of Australia, Durkheim discovered that the moral law of the tribe was to teach to youngmen in the very sacred ceremonies known as initiation ceremonies. On the sacred ceremonial ground where these initiations take place, various rites are performed which he called sacred and constituted essential part of the religion. Some of the profane activities, i.e., non-sacred activities are forbidden on these occasions, which Durkheim suggested antithesis of sacred. Thus, opposite of sacred is profane.

However, in the study of Indian civilization specially while studying the Hindu places of pilgrimage in terms of "Sacred Complex", (Vidyarthi 1961, Jha 1971, Vidyarthi, Saraswati and Jha 1979, etc.,) the concept of sacred has been applied differently from Durkheim's views of sacred and profane, as referred to above.

Difference between Magic, Religion and Science

James Frazer in his book *Golden Bough* made a detail analysis of magic and religion. As he was a classical evolutionist (Jha, 1983, 1994) he attempted to explain the evolution of culture through the evolution of magic, religion and science.

As Tylor made an attempt to explain evolution of culture from *savagery to barbarism* and then finally to civilization, similarly, Frazer suggested that when there was period of savagery, it was the stage of development of magical rites and practices. Again, when there was a stage of barbarism as suggested by Tylor, it was the period of development of religious rites and practices according to Frazer. However, the period of civilization is compared with the period of science by Frazer. This may be demonstrated through a diagram.

Evolution of Culture, Religion & Science:
  According to Tylor -   According to Frazer
  ↑ Civilization   -   Science   ↑
  ↑ Barbarism   -   Religion   ↑
     Savagery   -   Magic

Thus, from the evolutionary point of view, magic, religion and science have been evolved according to the corresponding stages of savagery, barbarism and civilization. Both Tylor and Frazer are universally accepted as the classical evolutionists.

However, from the functional point of view, Malinowski's book Magic, Science and Religion (1925) is an excellent attempt to throw light on the differences between these three important phenomenas. In the same year R.H. Lowie's book—*Primitive Religion* (1925) was also published who provided many theoretical insides of primitive magic and religion.

According to Frazer, "Magic is the bastard sister of science". He suggested that in scientific analysis "cause and effect" works together but in magical rites which are practiced indirectly, usually in darkness, are not to be observed by the public as in the case of physical sciences. Hence, magical rites are called pseudo-science. Frazer has suggested that, broadly, speaking magic may be categorised into two categories: Homeopathic magic and contagious magic. On the basis of evidences collected from different parts of the world Frazer found that magical formulae are based on two main principles:

(a) Like produces like, which means "Law of similairty" and the magic associated with it is called *Homeopathic magic* or *imitiative magic* or *mimetic magic*. (b) And, the second was called by him the *Law of contact* or *contagious* and the magic associated with it was called *contagious magic*. On these two principles are based all the various magical rites found in primitive society. All types of magic were called by Frazer *sympathetic* because he considered them to be based on the principles of sympathy between cause and effect.

Difference between Magic and Science

There are many differences between science and magic.

Comparing magic with science, Frazer writes "magic's fundamental conception is identical with that of modern science, underline the whole system is a faith implicit but a real and firm in the order and uniformity of nature". The magician does not doubt even for a single moment that the same causes will always produce with the effects, that the performances of the proper ceremony accompanied by the appropriate skill will inevitably be attended by the desired wishes unless indeed his incontinence should chance to be thwarted and foiled by more important charms of another sorcerers. Again, there is much conformity between magic and science in Frazer's opinion as far as the basic principles of operation are concerned. Both magic and science involve a belief in the "necessary causality" in all events. This is also the universal law of nature on which the science of logic is based. It involves a principle of association. The analogy between the magical and scientific conception of the world is enclosed. In both of them, the succession of event is perfectly regular and certain. Being determined by the immitable laws, the operation of which can be foreseen and calculated precisely. Both of them opened up a seemingly boundless vista of possibilities to him who knows the cause of things and can touch the sacred objects. Hence, the strong attraction with magic and science alike have exercised on the human mind and hence the powerful stimulus both have given to the pursuit of knowledge.

However, there are some basic differences between science and magic which may be noted below:

Science	Magic
1. Science is guided by reason and corrected by observation.	Magic lives in an atmosphere of mysticism.
2. Science is born of experiences.	Magic is based on tradition.
3. Science is open to all, for common good of the society.	While magic is an occult and it is taught through mysterious institution and initiations.
4. While science is based on the conceptions of natural forces.	Magic springs from idea of certain mystic, impersonal power, which is believed by primitive people.

Magic and Religion

According to Frazer both magic and religion are tools of adaptation and the object is to help man out of different situation and relieve his tension. In this connection it has to be mentioned here that both magic and religion have existed in the society since time immemorial. However, the magical approach is more primitive, while the religion's approach is comparatively refined and direct.

There are some differences between religion and magic, which are noted below precisely for the benefit of the students.

Religion	Magic
1. Religion is public and communal	Magic is confined to an individual.
2. Religion has a congregational aspect.	Air of secrecy surrounds the magician.
3. While in religion, priest commands respect in the society.	But the magician is very much feared in the society.
4. While priest in considered benevolent.	Magician is considered malevolent and harmful for the society.

However, at the same time there are some similarities also between religion and magic. For instance, both the priests and the magicians mediate between this world and the unseen world. As in religion, one cannot reach the god without the help of the priest, so also without the help of the magician one cannot propitiate any magical performance. With such a viewpoint and with absolute confidence Frazer stressed the role of magic in society and its relation to religion. The magician's art and religion's rituals, both are meant to create an atmosphere of suggestibility, and the technique employed by both is, more or less, similar. The performance of both is governed by traditional order and, conformity to which is essential for success. Magic and religion serve the same purpose, viz., that of restoring confidence in times of danger and crises. When magic fails repeatedly religion helps and both may often jointly contribute towards tiding over social and economic crises. In the normal day to day life of primitive man there may or may not be any mystery, but in his sleep and in times of impending danger, mystery is associated with his experience, so that he combines his fear and hope with the concept of supernaturalism.

Totem and Taboos

The study of totem and taboos attracted the attention of many British scholars in the last century but its scientific study was made by Radcliffe Brown, Golden Weiser, etc., in detail. Generally, when we refer to totemism, we mean that a tribe has a social organisation, usually of the sib or clan pattern, which is associated with a form of supernaturalism consisting of certain typical attitude towards species of animals or plants or classes of natural objects. Thus, the study of totem is related to both religion and social organisation.

Therefore, it is said that totemism has two broad aspects, first, a social aspect and secondly, a religious aspect or ritual aspect. What is referred to as social aspect of totemism is simply the clan organisation. But exogamous clan similar in all essentials to totemic clans so far as economic or judicial functions go, can exist without totemism? The so-called social aspect of the clan totemism is simple. The social aspect of the totemism is usually referred to as clan totemism. In clan totemism, there may be either matrilineal clan totemism or patrilineal clan totemism. In addition to it, there may be individual or personal totemism. This is a special relation between an individual and some one or more species of animals. A typical example of this type is the magician who must have a personal totem which he worships sometime in public or sometime separately in privacy.

Among the Indian tribes, there are many examples of totemic exogamous clan, some of which may be cited here for the benefit of the students. Among the Kharia tribe, there are many totemic exagamous clan, and there is a feeling of solidarity among the clan men. The Kamar tribe has also a clans-based totemic association of the animals, such as tiger, snake, tortoise, etc. Among the Ollar-Gadba, the phratries are divided among a number of totemic animals such as—*Meena-bansha* (fish), *Nag-bansha* (Cobra) and *Bagh-bansha* (Tiger), etc.

So far as, the religious aspect of totem is concerned, many scholars like Tylor, Durkheim, etc., wrote vividly on this subject. Durkheim saw in totemism the collective emblem of the society and hence he suggested that the totemic worship is really the worship of the society. While Tylor suggested that totemism emerged in the form of religious worship and the concept of ancestor-worship has been derived from the religious aspect of the totemism objects.

There are other scholars such as, Boas, Swanton, etc., who regarded totemism as an extension of the personal relation of an individual with an animal and plant. Thus, the dyadic relationship between totem and totemic object has been explained and examined from different angles. Golden-Weiser was of the opinion that there cannot be a particular object for the riddle of totemism. According to him neither it is useful nor it is uniform in every tribal society. Because the concept of totemism varies and differs from place to place as well as from tribe to tribe. However, Golden-Weiser regarded it as a socio-religious institutions and suggested that the totemism does play some important role in the existence of such peculiar institution.

Herbert Risley, who collected data from Indian tribes, said that in India the religious aspect of totemism is almost dead to a considerable extent, and the social aspect is more operative. Another important aspect of Indian totemism, as has been reported by a number of ethnographers, is accidental connection between a group of animal or plant-species and the tribal people. Elwin has reported that totemism may be the outcome of an historical accident or imitation. For instance, a man may kill a snake and later on, he was afflicted with blindness and he would have consulted the medicine man, the later would have certainly linked the two incidents. Consequently, the sufferer would develop a reverential attitude towards all the snakes and in course of time, he would worship the snakes and protected them.

The origin and development of the totemic groups has also been explained by S.C. Roy, the father of Indian Anthropology, in connection with the *Oraon Religion and Customs (1928)*.

Roy has suggested that *Fusion, Fission* and generalisations factors are responsible for the growth of totemic clans. By *fusion*, he meant coming to-gether of several families and adopting a common name which later on became a totemic emblem. By *fission*, he meant that sometime a clan may become of very large size, and in course of time that clan may split into various smaller groups and that process should be called as the process of fission. If the original clan has been called as tiger's tail, the latter would be called tiger's claw, or tiger's teeth and so on. By generalisation process, Roy meant that sometime it may happen that a person is protected or harmed by a tree or an animal and consequently, he would develop, a special attitude of friendly gratitude or reverence towards the animals or the tree. Later on, his descendants may continue special relation. Hence, according to Roy, the generalisation process would explain sometime, the emergence of totemism.

Majumdar while working among the Ho tribe of Chotanagpur, suggested that in most cases, it was an accidental relationship between the individual and the plant or an animal which was later on generalized. Huttan believes that beginning of this institution at a particular time may be slender, but in course of time all sorts of secondary reasons might contribute to the strength of the institutions. One of the most significant of these secondary causes is the need of maintaining an ecological balance, a simple adjustment of man-nature relationship, as has been explained by Vidyarthi (1963), which could bring about a sympathetic relationship betwen man and his environment leading to totemism on the social level.

Radcliffe Brown in his paper on the *"Sociological Theory of Totemism"* (Fourth Pacific Science Congress, Java, 1929), suggested two very important words regarding the totemism, (a) Ritual relations between persons and their totems, and (b) Ritual attitude, where every society adopts and imposes upon its members certain objects and this attitude of mind and behaviour, according to Radcliffe Brown, is called the ritual attitude. He pointed out that the ritual attitude may vary from a very indefinite one to a definite, and highly organised one. But all the varieties have something in common, shared by the members or sections of the society. The primary object of the ritual attitude is a social order and that anything becomes an object of that attitude when it stands in certain relation to the social order. A social group such as a clan can only possess and create solidarity, if it is the object of sentiments or attachments in the minds of the members and, hence, there must be a collective expression. Totems, as a matter of fact, create a national solidarity among the tribes as well as social and religious solidarities.

There are some tribes in the world where totems are absent and among non-totemic tribes special mention may be made of the Andman Islanders, the Eskimo, etc.

Like totem, taboo is not an English word. The word "taboo" has been derived from the Polynesian word *tabu*, which means to forbid or forbidden. Taboo is used to designate all the restrictions communicated through verbal *don't do* and is generally associated with the ritualistic behaviour.

Taboo has been called the unwritten law of the savage society and its violation is dealt by the council of elders.

James Frazer was the first scholar to investigate about the taboo and he wrote the article on taboo for the 9th edition of the Encyclopaedia Britanica. He, for the first time, started studying the concept of taboo as early as in 1986.

Radcliffe Brown has proposed the word *"Ritual avoidance"* or *"ritual prohibitions"* and attempted to define it by a reference of two fundamental concepts, i.e., *"ritual status"* and *"ritual value"*. According to him *"ritual prohibitions"* is a rule of behaviour which is associated with a belief that an infraction will result in the ritual status of the person who fails to keep the rule".

There are different types of taboos prevalent in the tribal society. Some of these taboos are—the *productive taboo*, the *protective taboo*, the *prohibited taboo,* etc. Productive taboo is associated with the process of cultivation, while the protective taboo is maintained in order to get protection from dangerous animals. The prohibited taboo is practised when members of the society are called or adviced to keep a distance from such plants and animals in order to keep a limited contact.

In tribal societies taboo is practiced in different spheres of life. For example, the food taboo, for cutting a particular plant or killing a particular totemic animal, etc. Those persons whose totem is *Bagh* (tiger), they would never kill the tiger. On occasions when the tiger would roar in the jungles, those persons would bow after hearing the roaring sound. Similarly, the members of the cobra clan would never kill the cobra and hence taboo is practiced in killing the cobra. The members of the tortoise clan would never eat the tortoise and they would never kill their totemic emblem. In this way avoidance of food related to totem is practiced in the tribal societies to a great extent. In this way it can be concluded that the concepts of totem and taboo, as practiced among the tribes of the world, provide them a sense of confidence, comfort, and a sense of socio-religious security. By practicing it, they become free from fears and anxieties.

CHAPTER VIII

Field-Work And Field-Work Traditions in Anthropology

Importance of Field-Work in Anthropology

Anthropology is a field-science and field-work is an integral part of this discipline. The early anthropologists, specially the classical evolutionists did not collect the scientific data by conducting field-work. They depended on the travellers, traders and missionaries who supplied them informations on the curious customs of the savages. And that's why their data were based on secondary sources and their findings were mostly conjectural.

However, when anthropology as a separate discipline of teaching and research was started in some of the European and American Universities in the late half of the 19th century, the importance of carrying out empirical field-work became compulsory. In the beginning, descriptive ethnographic works were taken up and the simple monographs were written by the early ethnographers.

Ethnographic field-work is a research carried out by the anthropologists among the living peoples in different parts of the world. It is generally undertaken to collect basic ethnographic data on a little known society or sub-society. In some of the ethnographic researches some theoretical aims are also examined, besides the descriptive nature of the research work. In many ways the beginning of field-work is a most difficult part of the research. Many serious problems can occur during the first few weeks in the field. First, there is a problem of initial impression one creates during the first meeting before the members of the society or sub-society one is studying. The problem is greatest among the inaccessible tribal societies where the group is small and the stranger is seen as a potential threat to the group.

Entry into the community necessitates the establishment of a good support. The role one assumes at the beginning of the field-work can affect research work during the later stages of the field-work. The researchers sometimes experience "culture shock" and they become disoriented when they realise that the people they are studying operate by a different set of cultural rules. Culture shock usually has only a temporary effect. However, after a few days of depression the researcher is now able to take up the field-work seriously. The researcher who is not fluent in the language of the native, faces some problem in the beginning.

As field-work is a compulsory paper in the curriculum of anthropology and sociology of the most of the universities of India, field-work is done by the students under the supervision of a teacher who imparts knowledge of the theory, model, designs of research, application of research methods, selection of appropriate topics of research, creation of specific aims, objectives and hypothesises, etc. All these preparations are done at the preliminary stage when some relevant books concerning the research topics are also consulted. However, after doing all these preparations at the headquarters, one now leaves for the field for conducting researches.

Field-Work Tradition in Anthropology

Anthropological expeditions began in America with the work of Boas in Baffin Land and British Columbia where he studied the Kwakiutl Indians, the Eskimo, etc. and were initiated in England shortly afterwards by Haddon of Cambridge, who led a band of scholars to conduct research in the Torres Straits region of the Pacific in 1898 and 1899. This expedition marked a turning point in the history of anthropology in Great Britain. From this time two important inter-connected developments began to take place. Anthropology became more and more a whole-time professional study and some field-experiences came to be regarded as an essential part of the training of its students.

As pointed out earlier, the early professional field-worker had many weaknesses. However, the scholars who carried it out might have been trained in other subjects of interest and came to anthropology out of curiosity. For example, Maine, MacLennan, Bachofen, Morgan, etc., among the earlier anthropological writers were lawyers; Spencer was a philosopher, Tylor was a curator, Pitt Rivers was a soldier, Lubbock was a banker, Robertson Smith was a Minister and a Biblical scholar and Frazer was a classical scholar. Again, the men who became eminent anthropologists of the world in the early part of the present century were mostly the natural scientists. Boas, who became a founding teacher of anthropology in the Columbia University, U.S.A. in 1896, was a scholar of physics and geography. Haddon was a marine geologist and Rivers was a physiologist. Seligman was a pathologist, Elliot Smith an anatomist, Malinowski a scholar of physics and Radcliffe Brown, though he had taken the moral sciences Tripos at Cambridge, had also been trained in experimental psychology. These men, who had training in other subjects, became world-famed scholars in anthropology by doing excellent field-work in anthropology. However, the most important of these was work of Radcliffe Brown and Malinowski. Radcliffe Brown, a student of Rivers and Haddon in Cambridge, went to study the Andaman Islanders from 1906 to 1908. It was a first attempt by a social anthropologist to investigate sociological theories in a primitive society and to describe the social life of the people in such a way as to bring out clearly what was significant in it for those theories. In this connection it may be pointed out here that the field-work expedition of Radcliffe Brown was perhaps of better importance in the history of field-work tradition in anthropology than Torres Straits expedition, carried out by Haddon.

Malinowski, the people of Hobhouse, Westermarc and Seligman, carried out field research a step further. If Radcliffe Brown has always had a wider knowledge of general social anthropology and has proved himself a master-mind thinker, Malinowski was the more through field-worker. He not only spent a longer period than any anthropologists before him and I think after him also, in a single study of a primitive people, the Trobriand Islanders of Malanesia between 1914 and 1918, but he was also the first anthropologist to conduct his research through the native language, as he was the first to live through out his work in the centre of native life. In these favourable circumstances, Malinowski collected a bulk of data on the life of the natives and wrote not only several excellent monographs but also developed his theory of functionalism and became champion of functional school of thought.

Some of the British anthropologists and other scholars pursued this tradition of field-work and studied a number of tribes of Africa and produced first-hand monographs. Among these scholars, special mention may be made of Evans-Pritchard's work on the Azande of the Anglo-Egyptian Sudan and Nuer, Nadel's account of the Tallensy of the Gold-coast, Kuper's account of the Swazi, Schapera's account of the Bechuana.

Besides these important works of British scholars based on empirical field-works, some of the American anthropologists, who were mostly the students of Franz Boas created a healthy trend of field-work in anthropology. Among such scholar, special mention may be made of A.L. Kroeber, Clark Wissler, R.H. Lowie, Ruth Benedict, Margaret Mead, etc., who have produced excellent analytical works based on intensive field-work carried out in different parts of the world.

In India, when the teaching of anthropology at the post-graduate level was started in 1920, a curriculum for intensive field-work was also chalked out. Among those early Indian anthropologists who did pioneering field-works among different tribal societies of India, special mention may be made of K.P. Chattopadhyay, T.C. Das, D.N. Majumdar, N.K. Bose, A. Aiyappan, Balakrishnan Aiyer, etc. These scholars carried out intensive field-works among the tribal societies of India. Again, G.S. Ghurye of Bombay University not only studied tribes and castes of India, but also studied the Indian *Sadhus* (ascetics) and set a new-trend of research in Indian sociology and social anthropology. Later on M.N. Srinivas studied the Coorgs of Rampura village very intensively and significant concepts were developed, which are still in vogue today and these are considered to be the significant land marks in Indian anthropological researches. In this connection the works of S.C. Dube, B.K. Roy Burman, Surjit Chandra Sinha, L.K. Mahapatra, P.K. Bhowmick, L.P. Vidyarthi, T.B. Nayak, B.N. Saraswati, N.K. Behura, etc., which are based on extensive field-works are the guide-lines of future trend of research work in Indian anthropology. Further, some of the anthropologists of the younger generation have also done extensive field-work both in India and other neighbouring countries. Among these younger generations of anthropologists special mention may be made of M. Jha's area of field investigation, extended from the high Himalayas of Garhwal and Kumoan in India and Kathmandu in Nepal in the North to Lakshadweep Islands in the south and from Gujarat in the west to the Kamakhya, Assam in the east. Based on the extensive field-works, Jha has produced dozens of excellent analytical works in Indian anthropology. Similariy, A.C. Sinha has done extensive field-work in Sikkim and Bhutan and has written several analytical books, based on empirical field-work. A.K. Danda and R.S. Mann have also done extensive field-work and have enriched the Indian anthropology.

Thus, both at the global level as well as the national level, field-work traditions in anthropology have been considered to be an integral part of this discipline. Of late, field-work traditions have been accelerated by many research innovations specially in the area of field methods and methodology.

Approaches in Anthropological Field-Work

In anthropological field-work various approaches are applied to collect data and make analysis of the scientific materials. Some of the important approaches are described below, in brief, for the benefit of the students.

(i) Synchronic Approach

Synchronic approach is based on empirical field-work where from the first-hand data are collected. The ethnographic details as well as the analytical details are analysed in terms of the empirical materials. The nineteenth century scholars of the early anthropologists never applied the synchronic approach to study the primitive people. As referred to earlier, they depended too much on the secondary sources.

(ii) Dychronic Approach

This approach is not based on field-work, rather it is based on the written documents or other indirect materials, of course, which are relevant for the concerned research work. Some materials are collected through the library work.

However, usually in carrying out a research work a researcher usualy combines both the approaches to write a balanced report usually from an analytical point of view.

(iii) Inductive and Deductive Approach

In anthropology usually the unit of study is always small, say a village, a particular tribe or caste, etc. By studying a village the researcher throws light on the wider perspective of the subject. The most befitting example of this approach is Dube's book—*Indian Village* (1955), which is based on the study of a village named *Shamir Peth,* located in Telangana near Hyderabad.

The inductive approach is very popular in anthropological researches. As mentioned above, the unit of research is very small and conclusions are drawn on a bigger scale. The word "inductive" has been derived from logic where it is said:

Ram is mortal,
Shyam is mortal,
Therefore, all men are mortal.

Thus, conclusions have been drawn at the very wider level while the unit of study is small. This is applied in anthropological researches too.

The word, deductive has also been derived from the logic where the situation is just reverse than the inductive approach. Thus, in the deductive approach the unit of study in very big but the conclusions are drawn at a very small level: say;

All men are mortal,
Ram is a man,

Therefore, Ram is mortal.

Thus, in anthropological researches also, when we take up a bigger unit of study, say, country as a unit of study, and conclusions are drawn at the very general or smaller level, we may call it a deductive approach. This approach, however, is not very popular in anthropological study.

(iv) Textual and Contextual Approach

The textual approach is based on the study of textual references concerning work. For example, in the study of sacred complexes of Hindu Tirthas (places of pilgrimage), the textual approach becomes an essential part of the research work. When Vidyarthi studied the *Sacred Complex of Hindu, Gaya* (1961), he first, read several *Purans* in which the myths and *mahatms* had been described and thereafter, he collected the field materials. Similarly, in the study of the *Sacred Complex of Kasi* (1979), the authors (Vidyarthi, Saraswati and Jha), consulted many *Purans* and other historical documents, besides the empirical field-work. Thus, textual approach becomes necessary not only in the study of Indian civilization but also in the study of culture change and other analytical and problem-oriented research work where bench-line-data are to be consulted in order to explain the field-data.

The contextual approach is like a synchronic approach which is based on empirical field-work. The contextual approach is applied in the field to collect first-hand data by applying the different field methods.

(v) Etic and Emic Approach

Etic is a level for a variety of theoretical approaches in anthropology concerned with the outsiders view of culture. Etic involves the careful specifications of the categories, the logical relations between categories and assumptions underlying the uses of these categories by social scientists. In brief, however, it may be said, when an outsider studies the culture with special reference to the natives language, it is called an etic approach.

Emic approach refers to a variety of theoretical field

approaches in anthropology concerned with the inside or native view of a culture. This concept was developed by Kenneth Pike (1954). Thus, in the emic approach the researcher usually presents the insiders' view.

(vi) Micro-Macro Approach

This approach is like inductive-deductive approach as mentioned earlier. This approach is applied in the field of planning and launching the developmental scheme. Vidyarthi has suggested that in the flied of applied anthropology and specially for the tribal development, planning and programmes should be chalked out at the local level, what he called micro-level; at the regional level which he called meso-level and the programme at the national level was called by him as the macro-level. However, in anthropological researches also some anthropologists are making an attempt to apply these approaches.

In brief, it may be said that all these various approaches cannot be applied simultaneously by the researcher. The success of the research and scientific desired results depend on the suitability of the approaches to be applied by the researchers in relevance of his research programmes. The themes, issues, aims and objectives of the research programmes or different hypothesis, if raised any, etc., are all to be considered by the researcher at the time of selecting the appropriate approach relevant to his anthropological investigations.

Definition of Hypothesis and Methodology

The anthropological researches, have been popular, though not unhealthy prejudiced against theories and contrasted with experience. However, an established theory is only a generalisation from experience which has been again confirmed by the anthropological field study.

Research methodology, as a matter of fact, includes everything concerning the research. However, I may demonstrate it in a tabular form.

```
                    Research Methodology
         ┌───────────────────┴───────────────────┐
    Research Methods                      Forms of Thought.
    or Field Techniques.                  It includes research designs,
                                          formulation of hypothesis,
                                          if any, aims and objectives,
                                          selection of suitable
                                          approaches etc.
```

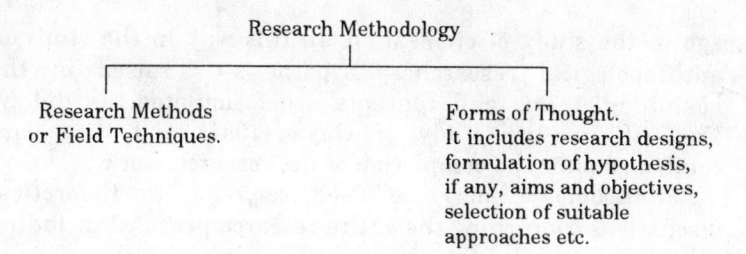

I now discuss below the definitions of hypothesis and research methodology, precisely, for the benefit of the students.

A hypothesis is usually defined merely as an unconfirmed opinion, that judging by what is already known it is reasonable to assume that further facts will be found by the researcher to support it or to reject it. By citing an example from my own study, I may make it more clear. In the study of the *Sacred Complex of Janakpur* (1971), it was a hypothesis that "the boundary of a civilization is not always the boundary of a nation" which I had raised at the time of formulating the research project. After the study was over and the results were published, it was successfully found that this hypothesis was true, which was confirmed by the empirical study.

In 1954, Milton Singer came to India to study the various dimensions of Indian civilization. When he came here, he raised a hypothesis that "in a primary civilization like India, cultural continuity with the past is so great that the conceptions of modernizing and progress ideologies does not result in linear forms of social and cultural change but may result in the traditionalizing of apparently modern innovations". In the light of this broad, based hypothesis, it was found that in India our cultural continuity with the past is really so strong that whenever any road is constructed, it is named after our great ancient hero or after any God or Goddesses, say the Maha Rana Pratap Road, or Man Singh Road etc. This hypothesis was further tested in the study of Janakpur, Nepal, by Jha (1971), when he found that some of the cinema halls, rice-mills, etc., had been named as Hanuman Cinema Hall, Janaki Rice Mill, etc., and all these go to confirm the hypothesis raised by Milton Singer, long ago in the study of civilization. In this way in the study of anthropological researches, hypothesis is raised in the beginning, terms and concepts are formulated, as did by Vidyarthi in the study of Gaya (1961) and those are confirmed after the completion of the research work.

"Methodology" may be used to refer to theorctical discussions concerning the entire research proposal including the forms of thought of the research, aims and objectives of the research, application of the research methods, etc. Thus, a distinction must be made between methods and methodology. By the word method, we mean usually the several research methods like interview method or observation method or G.T. method, etc., but when we refer to the word "Methodology", we mean the entire syllabus of the research activities including the application of the research techniques. In other words, the methodology carries a broad meaning and may be used to designate specially the analytical discussions of various research methods, which fall within the ambit of methodology.

"Methodology" is also often used in a narrow sense to refer to the methods, techniques or tools, employed for the collection and processing of data. But in a broader sense methods or techniques are one of the components of methodology. Finally, methodology may be called to designate all the concepts and procedures employed in the analysis of data, however, collected to arrive at conclusion.

Field-Methods in Anthropology

In anthropology, there are various fields methods or field techniques through which the scientific field data are collected. Some of the important field methods are mentioned below, for the benefit of the students.

(a) Interview Method

This is a very simple anthropological method which is applied by the researcher to collect data. However, selection of the information is very important. An informant should be a reasonable man, who is aware of all the happenings taking place around him. Thus, he should be a knowledgeable man.

Interview Method is of different types such as:

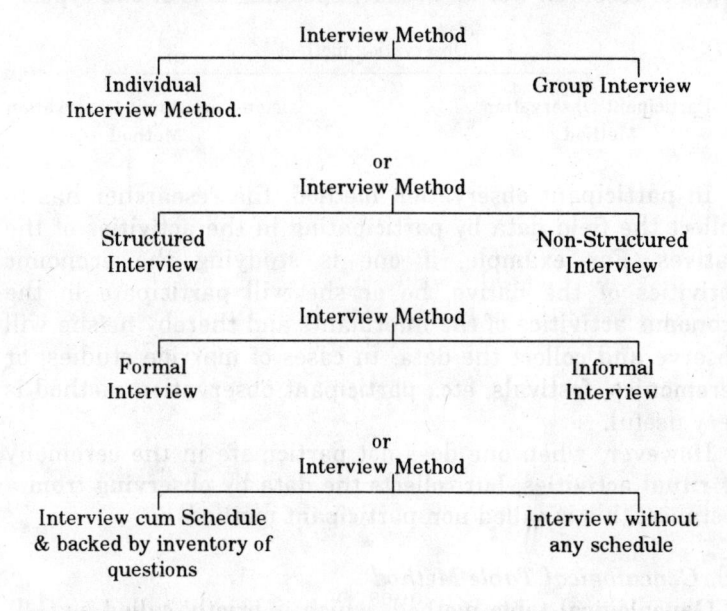

```
              Interview Method
              ┌──────┴──────┐
      Individual         Group Interview
   Interview Method.
```

```
                    or
              Interview Method
              ┌──────┴──────┐
       Structured         Non-Structured
       Interview           Interview
```

```
              Interview Method
              ┌──────┴──────┐
         Formal              Informal
       Interview             Interview
```

```
                    or
              Interview Method
              ┌──────┴──────┐
   Interview cum Schedule    Interview without
   & backed by inventory of    any schedule
        questions
```

According to the length of Time:

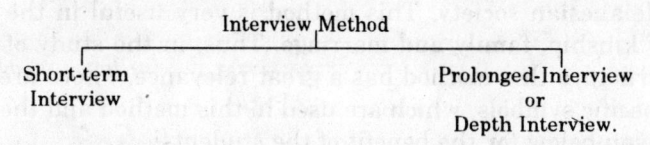

```
              Interview Method
              ┌──────┴──────┐
       Short-term          Prolonged-Interview
       Interview                  or
                           Depth Interview.
```

From the pathological point of view:

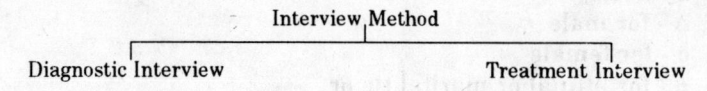

```
              Interview Method
              ┌──────┴──────┐
    Diagnostic Interview    Treatment Interview
```

Thus, there are various types of the Interview Method and the relevance of its application in the field depends on the nature of research one is conducting. An interview is thus, an oral type of questionnaire in which the interviewee gives the needed information in a face to face relationship.

(b) Observation Method

Observation method is also equally suitable for different

types of research works. Broadly speaking it is of two types:

```
              Observation method
    ┌──────────────┴──────────────┐
Participant Observation    Non-Participant Observation
    Method.                        Method.
```

In participant observation method, the researcher has to collect the field data by participating in the activities of the natives. For example, if one is studying the economic activities of the native, he or she will participate in the economic activities of the informants and thereby he/she will observe and collect the data. In cases of marrige studies, or ceremonies, festivals, etc., participant observation method is very useful.

However, when one does not participate in the ceremony or ritual activities, but collects the data by observing from a distance, this is called non-participant method.

(c) Genealogical Table Method

Genealogical table method, which is briefly called as G.T. Method, was developed by W.H.R. Rivers in the study of the Melanesian society. This method is very useful in the study of kinship, family and marriage. Thus, in the study of social structure this method has a great relevance. There are some specific symbols, which are used in this method and these are given below for the benefit of the students:

Symbols:
Δ - for male
o - for female
= - for affinal or marital tie or
— - for consanguineal tie
I - for line of descent

The abbreviations used in the mapping of kinships are as follows:
Father = Fa
Mother = Mo
Husband = Hu

Wife = Wi
Brother = Br
Sister = So
Daugher = Da

For the benefit of the students, I draw below a G.T. of typical Nuclear family using the above symbols:

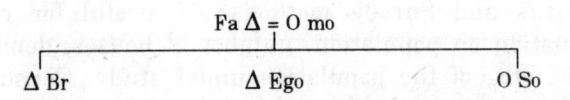

$$\text{Fa }\Delta = \text{O mo}$$
$$\Delta \text{ Br} \qquad \Delta \text{ Ego} \qquad \text{O So}$$

Ego is an important male or female informant through which the relation is traced in the genealogical table method.

(d) Schedule & Questionnaire Method

Schedule is an important research method which is applied in the collection of data in the field. Both schedule and questionnaire are used for the collection of personal references, social attitudes, beliefs, opinions, behaviour patterns, group practices and habits and such other information. The increasing use of schedule and questionnaire is probably due to increased emphasis by social scientists on quantitative measurements of uniformly accumulated data.

However, there is also difference between the schedule and questionnaire, although there are some similarities too. Both of them contain a large number of questions pertaining to the age, sex, name, caste and tribe, family members, economic status, etc., of the informant. But the differences lies in the mode of application of these two methods. While questionnaire is applied in the study of literate societies, specially in the study of impact of industrialization, urbanisation, etc., and it is filled up by the informant personally, schedule is usually applied by the anthropologists in the study of the primitive societies, which is filled up by the researcher personally after asking the question to the informants.

Schedules and questionnaires are beneficial as supplementary and extending devices in observations, in interviews, and in evaluating personal behaviour and social situations. They also aid in standardizing and objectifying observations and interviews and finally they are useful devices for isolating one element at a times and thus intensifying observation of it. The vast variety of schedule and questionnaire are prepared in detail for applying them in the large scale research project or in multidisciplinary research project.

(e) Census and Survey Methods

Census and Survey methods are useful for collecting information on population, number of houses, demographic details, etc., of the population under study. Census sheets usually contain basic biographical data like names, age, sex, kinship links, descent group, caste/tribe affiliation, past and present marriages, residential history as well as information on the educational background, occupation, income and other economic resources of the household members. Again, the researchers prepare the household survey from containing all these above mentioned details. The ethnographer's specific interests may add to this survey questions about rooming arrangements, health, problems, visiting facts and activities. Through census and survey methods a quantitative analysis of such data is made and the anthropologists/sociologists often detect underlying cultural regularities and obtain statistical measures in explaining the observed social processes.

(f) Sampling Method

Sampling method is applied when one is studying a very large population where census and survey of house to house are not possible to apply. Thus, sampling is done keeping in view the size of the population so that the proper representation of the people under study is made.

Sampling is of two types:- Random sampling and stratified sampling. In random sampling the researcher is free to apply sampling selecting the informants from different groups, but under stratified sampling, the population is stratified under different heads, viz., caste/tribe, age, sex, education, profession, economic status, etc., and thereafter the representational samples are selected for study.

In both the types of sampling methods statistical knowledge is required. Through the application of this method, quantitative data are usually collected and various diagrams and graphs are prepared to explain the sampling data. However, the impressionistic and qualitative facts are not explained through this method.

(g) Photographic and Cartographic Method

Due to development in the science and technology, different types of audio and video cassetes are applied to record the folk songs, dances and other details of folklore and life-styles of the people under study. The scientific development has given a rise to this method, which is now known as Visual anthropology.

Mapping involves the graphic recording of topographic and demographic data of the peopl'es environment. A map may contain the location of important natural resources: garden areas, forests, roads, paths, territorial/village boundaries, etc. Again, maps may detail, the layout of a typical house and the occupant's use of its quarters or the piece of land for cultivation, etc. In this way, the use of photographic methods, as well as the relevance and utility of the cartographic methods, have increased during the present day researches in social sciences.

(h) Psychological Method

With the growing importance of inter-disciplinary researches, anthropologists and psychologists have undertaken many research projects wherein psychological research methods are applied to study the personality formation, processes of socialization, etc.

Among the important psychological methods special mention may be made of the projective test, doll-painting, Rorschach test, etc. These methods are helpful for studying the colour blindness, attitude measurement, knowing the remembrance and memories, etc., of the people under study. With the help of psychological methods and anthropological approach, a new sub-discipline has emerged within anthropology, what is now known as Psychological anthropology.

(i) Contents Analysis Method

Contents analysis method was developed and applied for the first time during the Second World War when the first lady anthropologist of the world, Ruth Benedict was asked by the American authorities to study the Japanese from a distance. Thus, she studied the Japanese settled in U.S.A. through the contents published in the newspaper and arranged those contents in a meaningful way. Her important book—*Chrysanthemum And The Sword* (1946) is based on the content analysis method. This method is, thus, helpful in studying the patterns of behaviour of the people from a distance and where there is no possibility of conducting the field-work and collecting the first hand-information.

(j) Life History and Case Study Method

These two methods are very old in anthropology. When the informants are selected for depth interview, the researchers make a biographical analysis of the life-history of the informants. Usually the researcher gives emphasis as to how to get many insights and knowledge of the informants under interview. By studying the biographies of many informants, conclusions are drawn accordingly and this type of research is primarily based on life-history method. When cases of violation are noted specially in the cases of extra-martial relations in the society, or violation of incest-taboos, etc., cases are collected by the ethnographers to assess the quantum of stress and strain as well as the nature of disorganisation in the society.

(k) Formal Semantic Analysis Method

The formal semantic analysis method is also known as new ethnography. It has been developed recently and some anthropologists call it as componential analysis method. The formal semantic analysis method aims at making full and explicit accounts of the implicit knowledge people have about the cognitive (semantic) domains, i.e., about the knowledge which enables people to organise things in their world into systematic sets including part-whole relationships and hierarchically structured taxonomies. Some of the cognitive domains studied extensively or intensively are kinship terminology, colour-terminology, plant and animal taxonomies, food taxonomies, diagnostic taxonomies of disease and illness, etc. This research method is in vogue since last two decades and is being applied by the American anthropologists. However, in India M. Jha applied this method in the study of "Lakshadweep: Island Ecology and Cultural Perceptions" recently.

Creation of Rapport in Field-Work

When an anthropologist goes to conduct field-work in the remote areas, he remains all alone, cut off from the companionship of men of his own race and culture. He is then dependent on the natives around him for company, friendship and human understanding. Thus, an anthropologist has to create friendship and companionship in the field which will go a long-way to create rapport in the field. A field-worker usually carries with him some trophies and other small gifts for the children who flock around him. It is evident that he can only establish intimacy if he makes himself in some degree a member of the natives society and lives, thinks and feels in their culture since only he, and not they, can make the necessary transference. An anthropologist has failed, unless when he says goodbye to the natives there is on both sides the sorrow of parting.

In order to understand the native in totality, researcher should try to learn more and more about the native's language or dialect, their usual way of greeting their way of passing the leisure, etc., and try to mix up with them so intimately that the natives should understand the researcher as the member of their family. In this way, usually rapport is quickly created by the anthropologists in the field. In this way rapport creation is an integral part of the field-training in anthropology.

Some Important Literatures on the Field-Methods

There are many literatures published on different aspects of field-methods, some of which are mentioned below for the benefit of the students.

The British model of research is usually guided by the *Notes and Queries on Anthropology*. This is based on a big questionnaire framed more than hundred years ago by James Frazer, which was published as early as in 1874, since then it has undergone several editions.

The American model of research is based on *"Outline of Cultural Materials"*, which was also edited by an eminent American anthropologist several decades ago.

Besides these, there are a few more books on research methods, viz., "Scientific Social Surveys and Research" by P.V. Young (1968), "Field-Methods in Anthropology and other Social Sciences" by M.N. Basu (1961), "An Introduction to Research Procedure in Social Sciences" by M.H. Gopal (1964), "Methods of Social Research" by N.A. Thooti (1966), etc.

In Indian anthropology not much has been written on the research methods specially from the point of view of exploring the Indianness in Indian Social Sciences. However, a few books and some research papers have, of late, been published. A.K. Danda's book, "Research Methodology in Anthropology" (1992) is a useful text, which has come up recently. Earlier N.K. Bose (1968) had employed a geographical technique to present a micro-study of the process of urbanization in Calcutta. S.C. Dube (1955-1958) had pioneered group research in India and had also written about the methodological problems involved in it. Andre Beteille (1966) has given his reasons for underplaying the quantitative dimensions of social relations and Ram Krishna Mukherjee (1957) also highlights them.

A.K. Shah and R G. Shroff (1959) examined geneologies to reconstruct the social and economic history of the village under study. Similarly, Balley's attempt (1960) is an excellent example of the possibilities of the case study method. Vidyarthi (1961) was able to obtain much useful materials and gained good insights into the family life and the occupational culture of the Gayawals by collecting case studies. Similarly in the Study of Kashi (1979) the authors (Vidyarthi, Saraswati and Jha) collected more than twenty-seven life histories of the sacred specialists of Kashi to explain the insights and complexities of the culture of this great traditional city.

The importance of gearing social research to hypothesis-testing, generalization and prediction is stressed by Rama Krishna Mukherjee also. In various papers, such as "Some considerations on Social Researches (1960), "A Note on

Village as Unit" or "Variable for Studies of Rural Society" (1961), "On Classification of Family Structures" (1962) and "A Note on the measurement of Kinship Distance" (1963), he discusses when, how and why statistical concepts and tools should be employed in social research.

In this way several views have been expressed by the anthropologists and sociologists concerning the collection and interpretation of the data which the researcher faces both in the field as well as after return from the field. Madan (1965) has rightly said that an investigator faces the lack of social freedom both in collecting the data and interpreting them thereafter. However, application of methods in the field and analysis thereof depend upon the researcher as to how and from which angle he looks at and to what he wants to arrive at.

Bibliography

Baber, Ray.E.	1953:	Marriage and the Family, New York, Mc Graw Hill.
Basu, M.N.	1961:	Field Methods in Anthropology, and other Social Sciences; Book Land, Calcutta.
Beals, Ralph.L.	1969:	Politics of Social Research; Aldine Publishing Company, Chicago.
Beals and Hoijer	1956:	Introduction to Anthropology.
Bose.N.K.	1967:	"Some Methods of Studying Social Change" in *Man in India*, Vol 47, No-3.
Bohannan,N.P.	1963:	Social Anthropology; New York.
Bryson, Gladys.	1945:	Man and Society; Princeton.
Christensen, H.T.	1950:	Marriage Analysis; New York.
Durkheim, Emile	1912:	Elementary Forms of Religious Life; London.
Durkheim, Emile	1938:	The Rules of Sociological Method; Illinois.
Dube, S.C.	1952:	Social Anthropology; Hyderabad.
Dube, S.C.	1960:	Methodological Problems in Group Research, convention of Social Anthropologist; Lucknow.
Dube, Leela	1965:	"Training in Methods of Social Research"; in Sociology in India, Institute of Social Sciences, Agra.
Danda, A.K.	1992:	Research Methods in Anthropology, Inter-India Publications; New Delhi.
Einzig, Paul.	1935:	Primitive Money; London.
Elwin, Verrier	1941:	The Muria and Their Ghotul, London, Oxford University Press.
Elwin, Verrier	1955	The Religion of an Indian Tribe, London, Geofferey Cumberlege.

Evans, Pritchard, E.E.	1937:	Witch Craft, Oracles and Magic among the Azande, Oxford.
Evans, Pritchard, E.E.	1940:	The Nuer, Oxford.
Evans, Pritchard, E.E.	1951:	Social Anthropology; Cohen and West Ltd, London.
Evans, Pritchard, E.E.	1951:	Kinship and Marriage among the Nuer; London, Oxford University Press.
Eliade, Mircea (ed.)	1959:	History of Religions; Chicago.
Firth, Raymond	1953:	Elements of Social Organisation; London.
Perriera, J.V.	1965:	Totemism in India, Bombay, Oxford University Press.
Frazer, James, George	1910:	Totemism and Exogamy; (4 Vol,) London
Fraud, C.	1950:	Totem and Taboo; London, Hogarth Press
Geertz, C.	1962:	The Javanese Family, New York, Free Press.
Geertz, C.	1968:	"Religion As A Cultural System"; *in* Michael Banton, edited Anthropological Approaches to the Study of Religion, London, Tavistock Publication Ltd.
Ghurye, G.S.	1943:	The Aborigines So-called And Their Future; Poona, Gokhale Institute of Politics and Economics.
Ghurye, G.S.	1959:	The Scheduled Tribes, Bombay, Popular Book Depot.
Goode, William, J.	1951:	Religion in Primitive Society: Free Press.
Goode, William, J.	1965:	The Family; New York-Prentice Hall.
Goode, William, J. and Paul.K. Hall	1952:	Methods in Social Research; McGraw Hill, New York.
Jha, Makhan	1983:	An Introduction to Anthropological Thought; Vikas Publication, New-Delhi
Jha, Makhan	1983:	Reading in a Tribal Culture; Inter-India Publications, New Delhi.
Jha, Makhan	1992:	Lakshadweep: Sea Ecology and Cultural Perceptions; I.G.N.C.A, New Delhi.

BIBILOGRAPHY

Jha, Makhan	1994:	The Sacred Complex of Kathmandu, Nepal; Gyan Publication, New-Delhi.
Krishnarao, B.	1961:	The Descriptive Method In Social Research; Sociological Bulleti, 10 (2).
Lowie, R.H.	1920:	Primitive Society; London.
Lowie, R.H.	1924:	Primitive Religion; New York.
Maine, Henry.	1861:	Ancient Law; London.
Mc Lennan, G.F.	1865:	Primitive Marriage; London.
MacIver, R.M.	1937:	Society; London.
Malinowski, B.	1948:	Magic, Science and Religion and Other Essays; Glencoe (Illinois).
Marret, R.R.	1909:	The Threshold of Religion; London.
Morgan, Lewis.H.	1871:	Systems of Consanguinity and Affinity of the Human Family; Washington.
Morgan, Lewis.H.	1877:	Ancient Society; London.
Madge, John	1953:	The Tools of Social Sciences; Longman, Green and Co, London.
D.N. Mazumdar and T.N. Madan	1956:	An Introduction to Social Anthropology; Asia Publicating House, Bombay.
Murduck, G.P.	1968:	Social Structure; New York, The Macmillan and Co.
Nadel, S.F.	1951:	The Foundations of Social Anthropology; London, Cohen and West Co.
Nadel, S.F.	1957:	The Theory of Social Structure; Glencoe, Cohen and West Ltd.
Nimkoff, M.F.	1934:	The Family; Boston, Houghton, Mifflin Co.
Oommen, T.K.	1969:	Data Collection Techniques: The Case of Sociology and Social Anthropology; Economic and Political Weekly.
Piddington, Ralph	1950:	An Introduction to Social Anthropology (in two volumes); Edinburgh, Oliver and Boyd.
Radin, Paul.	1933:	The Method and Theory of Ethnology; New York.
Radcliffe, Brown, A.R.	1952:	Structure and Function in the Primitive Society; London.

Rivers, W.H.R.	1914:	Kinship and Social Organisation; London.
Royal Anthropological Institute of Great Britain and Ireland	1971:	Notes and Queries on Anthropology (6th Ed); Routledge and Kegan Paul Ltd, London.
Schapera, I.	1940:	Married Life in an African Tribe; Oxford.
Seligman, C.G. and B.Z.	1911:	The Veddas; Cambridge.
Sinha; Raghubir	1980:	Family to Religion; National Publishing House: New Delhi.
Saran, Gopala.	1983:	Sociology and Anthropology and other Essays; Institute of Social Research and Applied Anthropology, Calcutta.
Srinivas, M.N. (ED)	1960:	Method in Social Anthropology, Asia Publishing House, Bombay.
Saxsena, R.N.	1959:	Interdisciplinary Approach in Social Research; *in* Regional Seminar on Techniques of Research, UNESCO Research Centre, New-Delhi.
Thooti, N.A.	1966:	Methods of Social Research; Popular Prakashan, Bombay.
Verma, B.N.	1962:	The Role of Concepts and Models in Social Science; *in* B.N. Verma edited-A New Survey of the Social Sciences; Asia Publishing House, Bombay.
Vidyarthi, L.P.	1976:	Tribal Culture of India; Concept Publishing Co; New Delhi.
Vidyarthi, L.P.	1978:	Rise of Anthropology in India (two volumes); Concept Publishing Co; New Delhi.
Westermarck, Edward.	1891:	The History of Human Marriage; London.
Weber, Max.	1949:	The Methodology of Social Sciences; Free Press, Chicago.

Index

A Hundred years of Anthropology, 2
A Philosophy for NEFA, 15
Ackoff, 20
Aiyappan, A., 14-15, 146
Aiyer, Balakrishnan, 146
An Introduction to Research Procedure in Social Sciences, 160
An Introduction to Social Anthropology, 6
Animism, Tylor's theory of, 130-31
Anthropology,
    branches of, 3-16
    political, 112-24
Anthropology, 6
Archaelogical anthropology, 3
Associations, 28-30

Bachofen, 145
Balley, 160
Basu, M.N., 160
Behura, N.K., 147
Benedict, Ruth, 33, 146, 158
Bhowmick, P.K., 147
Bidney, David, 33
Birnbaum, 127
Biswas, 5
Blacksmith, 110
Boas, Franz, 2, 139, 144-45
Bose, N.N., 15, 146, 160
Buchanan, 14
Bucher, 108

Cardozo, 114
Chapple, 84
Chattopadhaya, K.P., 15, 146
Chandhari, Bundhadeb, 15
Chrysanthemum and the Sword, 158
Codrington, 132
Cognitive Anthropology, 11
Community, and society, 22-24, 26
Cooley, C.H., 23, 27-28, 30
Coon, 84

Custom and law, 115-16

Dalton, George, 14, 96-97
Danda, A.K., 147, 160
Darwin, charles, 3
Dey, S.K., 15
Dube, S.C., 6, 15, 147-48, 160
Durkheim, Emile, 5, 19, 63, 126, 128-29, 132-34, 139

Eastern Anthropologists, 15
Economic anthropology,
    definitions, 96-97
    meaning and scope, 94-96
    mode of exchange, 101-104
    primitive characteristics, 97-100
    characteristics, 107
    tribal market and trade, 105-06
Eggan, Fred, 18
Einzig, Pall, 106
Elementary Form of Religious Life, 133
Ellis, 110
Elwin, Verrier, 15, 83
Encyclopaedia of the Social Sciences, 2
Ethnology, 8
Evans-Pritchard, E.E., 5-6, 18, 62, 128, 146
Evolutionary anthropology, 4-7

Fallers, 66
Family,
    concept, 62-65
    definition, 65-67
    features, 64-65
    functions, 67-70
Fellow, Good, 96
Field Methods in Anthropology and Other Social Sciences, 160
Field Work in anthropology,
    importance of, 143-44

INDEX

traditions, 144-47
Firth, Raymond, 5, 20-21, 94-96
Folkways, 27
Fortes, M., 18
Frazer, James, 82, 126, 129, 134-37, 145, 159
Freud, Sigmund, 43, 82
Fried, Mortan, 25
Fuchs, 15

Geertz, 127
General Anthropology, 2, 7
Ghurye, G.S., 146
Ginsberg, M., 19
Gough, Kathleen, 41, 66
Green, A.W., 24, 27
Grigson, 14, 58
Groups type of, 30
Gurdon, 14

Haddon, 2, 144
Hammond, 59
Hawstrey, 110
Herkovits, M.J., 7
Herskovits, 2, 95, 97, 101
History of Human Marriage, 63
Hoebel, E.A., 2, 114, 117
Hutton, 140
Hypothesis and methodology, 150-52

Ideology and Utopia, 19
Indian Village, 148
Institutions, 26-28
Introduction to Anthropology, 7

Jacobs, M., 2, 7
Jevons, 106-07, 109
Jha, M., 62, 87, 99, 102, 134, 147, 151, 159-60
Justice and punishment in, primitive societies, 121-23
Kinship,
  amitate, 85
  avunculate, 85
  degree, 92-93
  descent rules of, 89-92
  groups, 77-81
  moiety, 86-89
Karve, Iravali, 60
Kluckhohn, 1-2
Kroeber, A.L., 33-34, 36, 146

Language, 10-11
Laum, 110-11

Leach, E.R., 5, 18, 66-67, 128
Levi-strauss, 18, 20, 22, 29
Levy, 66
Lindman, 23
Linguistic anthropology, 9-12
Linton, Ralph, 33, 65
Locke, 106
Lowie, R.H., 42-43, 65, 82, 86-87, 115, 131, 135, 146

MacIver, R.M., 19, 23-24, 27-28, 64
Maclennan, 145
Madan, 44, 55, 58-59, 96, 98, 115
Magic, concept of, 135-138
Magic Science and Religion, 135
Mahapatra, L.K., 147
Maine, Henry 117, 120, 145
Majumdar, D.N., 14-15, 44, 55, 58-59, 96, 98, 115, 132, 140, 146
Malinowski, Bronislaw, 5, 27-28, 32, 38, 43, 84-85, 95, 101-103, 126, 132-33, 135, 145-46
Man and His Works, 2,7
Man-in the Primitive World, 2
Mann, R.S., 147
Mannheim, K., 19
Mathur, 15
Marett, R.R., 126
Marriage,
  characteristics of, 42-45
  concepts, 39
  definitions, 40-41
  forms, 47-51
  hypergamy and hypogamy, 60
  mate acuqiring, 51-53
  rules, 57-60
Mead, Margaret, 33, 146
Menger, 106-109
Methods of Social Research, 160
Mill, John Stuart, 106
Mukherjee, Ram Krishna, 160
Muller, Max., 131-32
Murdock, G.P., 6, 40, 43, 65, 73-74, 87, 92
Nadel, S.F., 5-6, 18-19, 146
Naik, 15
Nation building process, 123-24
Naturalism, Max Muller's Theory of, 131-32
Nayak, T.B., 147
Nehru Jawaharlal, 15
Nimkoff, 23
Notes and Queries on Anthropology, 18, 159

Oraon Religion and Customs, 139
Orenstein, Henry, 15

Page, C.H., 19, 23, 27-28
Panunzio, C., 27
Parsons, Talcott, 25
Penniaman, T.K., 2
Physical anthropology, 3-4
Piddington, Ralph, 6, 96
Pike, Kenneth, 150
Political anthropology, 112-24
Primitive government, structure of, 118-20
Primitive law, 114-24
    custom and, 115-16
    definition, 114-15
    justice and punishment under, 121,24
    social sanctions in, 116-21
Principles of Sociology, 19

Radcliffe-Brown, A.R., 4-6, 18, 21, 132-33, 138, 140-41, 145
Raha, 15
Reasons and Unreason in Sociology, 19
Religion,
    anthropology of, 125-42
    meaning and people, 125-27
    taboos and totem, 138-42
    theories of, 129-34
Research Methodology in Anthropology, 160
Richards, Audrey, 44-45
Risley, Herbert, 14, 44, 139
Rites of Passage, 129
Rivers, Pitt, 145
Rivers, W.H.R., 86, 154
Ross, Edward, 30
Roy, S.C., 14-15, 83, 139-40
Roy-Burman, B.K., 15, 147

Sachchidanand, 15
Sacred and Profane, concepts, 133
Sacred Complex of Hindu Gaya, 149
Sacred Complex of Janakpur, 151
Sacred Complex of Kasi, 149
Sahlins, 95
Salisbury, 95
Saraswati, B.N., 134 147, 16>
Schapera, I., 5, 85, 146
Schumner, 30
Schurtz, 108
Science and magic, 135-36

Scientific Social Surveys and Research, 160
Seligman, 40, 145
Shell, 110
Shroff, R.G., 160
Singer, Milton, 35, 151
Sinha, D.P., 79, 105
Sinha, Surjit Chandra, 147
Slater, Marian, 43-44
Smith, Robertson, 126-145
Social and cultural anthropology, 4-8
Social organisation, 20-22
Social structure, 17-20
Society,
    characteristics of, 25-26
    community and, 22-24, 26
Society, 19
Sociological Thoery of Totemism, 140
Spencer, Herbert, 19, 145
Spiro, Melford, 66, 127, 129
Srinivas, M.N., 6, 146
State and Stateless political system, 120-21
Stephens, William N., 41, 167
Sumner, W.G., 27
Swanton, 139
Taboos and totem, 138-42
Taylor, E.B., 126
Threshold of Religion, 127
Toynbee, 35-36
Tribal Development in India: Problems and Prospects, 15-16
Tribal economy, 100-01
Tribal market and trade, 105-06
Tyler, Stephen A., 11
Tylor, E.B., 32, 43-44, 82, 85, 110, 126-28, 130-32, 134-35, 139, 145
    theory of animism, 130-31
Van Gennep, A., 129
Vidyarthi, L.P., 15, 89, 99, 121, 134, 140, 147, 149, 152, 160

Wald, Thuru, 108
Ward, 30
Weiser, Golden, 138-39
Wester marck, Edward, 40, 43-44, 63
Wilson, 97
Wissler, Clark, 146

Young, P.V., 160

Zimmerman, Carle C., 63
Zinsberg, 23-24